Old Barn Puppet Plays

Old Barn Puppet Plays

Seven Plans for 10-Minute
Puppetry Experiences
for Children 5–8

by
Taffy Jones

McFarland & Company, Inc., Publishers
Jefferson, North Carolina, and London

Photographs by Taffy Jones.
Big Barn designed and built by John Wessel, Little Barn designed and built by
Tina Clough.
Barnwell family dowel puppets designed by Lomie Larkin and illustrated by
Tina Clough.
"Scarecrows" stick puppets by Laurie Kapfer. Big Crow dowel puppet designed
by Lomie Larkin and illustrated by Tina Clough. Farmer Barnwell, Martha
Barnwell, and Gertie Goat stick puppets by Lomie Larkin.
"Gone Fishing" dowel puppets designed by Lomie Larkin and illustrated by
Tina Clough. Fish by Carol Pfenning.
"Camping Out" dowel puppets designed by Lomie Larkin and illustrated by
Tina Clough. Tent by Nancy Leinbach. Jelly bean cake designed by
Victoria Johnson and illustrated by Tina Clough.
"Who Stole the Pie?" dowel puppets designed by Lomie Larkin and illustrated
by Tina Clough. Blueberry pie designed by Lomie Larkin and illustrated
by Tina Clough.
"Froggie Woggies" stick puppets and "Monster Mosquito" created and illustrated
by Nori Hawkins. Water lilies by Nancy Leinbach.
"The Computer" dowel puppets designed by Lomie Larkin and illustrated by
Tina Clough. Computer drawing and directions by Nancy Leinbach.
Old Barn Invitation by Tina Clough.

Front cover: Young puppeteers enjoying their Barnwell family puppets. (Photo
by Taffy Jones.)
Back cover: Photograph of the author by Carol Tacea.

British Library Cataloguing-in-Publication data are available

Library of Congress Cataloguing-in-Publication Data

Jones, Taffy, 1922–
    Old barn puppet plays : seven plans for 10-minute puppetry
experiences for children 5–8 / by Taffy Jones.
        p.   cm.
    ISBN 0-7864-0327-6 (sewn softcover : 55# alkaline paper) ∞
    1. Puppet plays, American.   2. Puppet making.   3. Puppet theater.
I. Title.
PN1980.J57   1997
791.5'3'0973 — dc21   97-11198
                                                             CIP
                                                             AC

Manufactured in the United States of America

McFarland & Company, Inc., Publishers
    Box 611, Jefferson, North Carolina 28640

To my puppeteer grandson
Will Kapfer
with love and thanks

Acknowledgments

No way in Farmer Barnwell's great green acres is it possible to thank in print everyone who has helped to make *Old Barn Puppet Plays* a reality. So here and now, I say thank you to you *all*, with special thanks to:

Eunice Pomaville, who spent more time at the computer than Farmer Barnwell ever did.

Lomie Larkin, for her original and wonderful puppets and artwork.

Tina Clough for her fine artwork.

Nori Hawkins, who jumped right into the Froggie Wog pond with her frog puppets.

Laurie and Will Kapfer for their Scarecrows.

John Wessel for building a marvelous old barn that brought the plays to life.

Nancy Leinbach for her colorful backdrops and artwork.

Judy Wessel for typing and editing.

Betty Gunrud, children's librarian at the Tuftonboro Center School in New Hampshire, for digging out the weeds in the scripts and coming up with a super hoedown Foreword.

Gicele Perna (Miss Sally), children's librarian at the St. Lucie County Main System Library in Ft. Pierce, Florida, and *Kevin Berry*, library associate in youth services and puppeteering in Ft. Pierce, Florida.

Rosemarie Molea, educational consultant, and *John M. Harmes*, M.A., children's psychologist, who thought up the idea for the Talkabouts.

Thanks to you all!

Contents

Foreword

Whether they live on a farm or have never even seen one, all children will relate to the plays contained in this book. The characters are interesting and funny, and each play has something for everyone. The plays can be used for simple rainy day entertainment or for major productions. The book comes complete with scripts, detailed directions for scenery, and patterns for all of the puppets. It even shows how to make an easy and inexpensive Old Barn Theater, which will give your show a professional look.

There are recommended age groups for each play, but as you will know your cast best, you can pick and choose to suit their needs. Once the puppets and scenery have been made, your children can use them to branch out into other dramatic productions. The puppets and scenery lend themselves to many stories already known to children and will inspire them to create their own plays.

Taffy Jones suggests videotaping your sketches for later enjoyment by the cast and audience. This allows the children to be their own drama critics, enabling them to become better puppeteers and playwrights in the future.

Old Barn Puppet Plays is a valuable resource that can be used by the beginner as well as the veteran producer. The pictures are a great help to those who need a starting point to help them visualize and create on their own.

You will definitely enjoy this book. As they say on Broadway, "Break a leg!"

Betty Gunrud, Tuftonboro Center School Librarian
Center Tuftonboro, New Hampshire

Introduction

It is great fun living on an old farm and having your grandchildren play in the old barn.

Old Barn Puppet Plays was developed around the Joneses' 1869 farm and barn in New Hampshire. The puppet plays were presented in Melvin Village, New Hampshire, and in Fort Pierce, Florida.

Some puppet plays have been written in a simple style and the puppets are easy and inexpensive to make and to use. Other plays are more complicated, as are the puppets, to give the advanced puppeteers a chance to stretch their puppeteering skills and imagination.

The plays are for children 5 to 8 years, and each runs about 10 minutes long. The book contains patterns, photos and instructions for puppets, props, scenery and a barn theatre. The children can make their own puppets from the book to put on puppet plays at home or to present them before an audience. The more difficult puppets will need adult supervision in making.

It's best to choose the puppet voices by try-outs. Once they are chosen, you may prefer to tape your "voice actors" reading the lines, then play the tape while the puppeteers — who may or may not be the same children chosen as voice actors — operate the puppets. It is sometimes difficult for young children to speak lines and operate puppets at the same time.

The number of puppeteers needed depends on the skills of your group. Some children may be able to operate two puppets at once and even switch to other puppets as characters exit and enter. Other children may feel more comfortable working just one puppet throughout the play. At the end of the play, it is a nice gesture to have the puppeteers come out with their puppets to take a bow. It is also nice to have an announcer welcome the audience at the beginning.

3

The first of these plays is the easiest and can be performed and enjoyed by children as young as kindergarten age. The plays that follow tend to get progressively more complicated, but all can be enjoyed by all ages.

Some reminders for young puppeteers:

·Keep your puppet at the same height at all times.
·Speak in your puppet's voice, not your own voice.
·Watch that the puppets don't bump into each other.
·Keep your head and hands out of sight.
·Move only the puppet who is speaking; keep other puppets still.

It has been tremendously exciting and rewarding to work with all the Old Barn Puppets and the children who made and operated them. The children have related to these puppets as new friends and have enjoyed watching and performing the *Old Barn Puppet Plays*.

Happy Puppeteering!

Jaffy Jones

About the Talkabouts

Talkabouts are especially for the second and third grades, but kindergarteners and first graders can also answer easy questions about the plays. The teacher asks a question concerning the play just given, and the children talk about the question. Here are some questions to get started:

1. Did you like the story? Why or why not?
2. What was the play about?
3. Did you learn anything from seeing the play?
4. Would you like the play to end differently? How? Why?
5. Which puppet character did you like best? Why?
   Which puppet character did you not like? Why not?
6. Which puppet character would you like to be? Why?
   Which puppet character would you not like to be? Why not?
7. Do any of the puppet characters make you think of someone you know? Who?

There are Talkabouts at the end of every play for fun and learning.

How to Make an Old Barn Puppet Theater (Big or Small Version)

Big Version

To start the Old Barn, get the largest cardboard box you can find. (Try an appliance store.) The big barn in the photograph on the cover and on page 7 is 28" wide by 54" tall (not counting roof) by 14" deep; yours can be adjusted to suit your box size. With a sharp knife, cut an opening for the stage in front (the opening pictured on page 10 is 23" wide by 16" high). Remove the back of the box, leaving both sides attached; this will make it easy for puppeteers to come in and out. Now stand the barn upright. If it is a little wobbly, you can reinforce it with pieces of wood to make it stable enough to stay up during the performance.

You may feel like producing a puppet play right away with what you have already done. Go ahead and try it! The fancy stuff like the roof and curtain can be done at a later time.

The next thing you may decide to do is make the curtain. It is quite easy to do. Start with a ½" wood dowel long enough to span the stage opening with an inch of overlap on each side. Cut a piece of burlap or other strong cloth large enough to completely cover the stage opening, with at least a one-inch overlap all around, plus extra at the top. Wrap the material around the dowel at the top, then sew, or tack, or glue it in place.

Inside the theater, a bracket glued on each side of the stage opening will hold the dowel rod in place. You hang the curtain by placing

Farmer Barnwell and friend in front of small (left) and big versions of the Old Barn Puppet Theater.

the dowel in the brackets. Simply remove the curtain, dowel and all, to begin your play.

Backdrop curtains are made the same way and hung from brackets behind the stage area (the puppeteers work in front of these curtains). A backdrop remains in place throughout the scene, or even through the whole show, depending on the setting of the play.

To build the roof, use another large cardboard box. Cut a large triangle for the gable end. Glue a 4" strip of cardboard on each side of the bottom of this triangle, extending a couple of inches below the bottom. This will form a slot for sliding the gable onto the barn. (By using this arrangement you can easily remove the roof assembly for storage.) A thinner strip of cardboard about 10 or 11 inches wide may be bent over the gable and glued to it, with ends extending about an inch beyond the gable on either side, to make the roof itself.

Slide your new roof assembly onto the main body of the barn. Step back and take a proud look at your new creation. Looks good! Now you're ready to paint it. For an authentic look, try painting it red with a white trim. The result will be very pretty.

It is helpful to add a shelf inside the theater to serve as a stage floor. Plywood is a good choice. Cut a piece about seven inches wide and long enough to reach across the theater. Glue a strip of 1 × 1" wood to each inside wall, just below the stage opening, to support the shelf (see diagram on page 11).

If you really want to dress up your theater, a weathervane on the top is the perfect finishing touch.

The Big Barn Puppet Theater (designed by John Wessel)

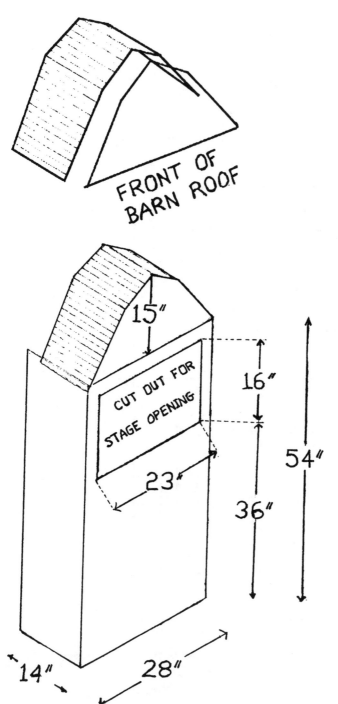

FRONT OF BARN ROOF

15"

CUT OUT FOR STAGE OPENING

16"

23"

54"

36"

14"   28"

Front of barn

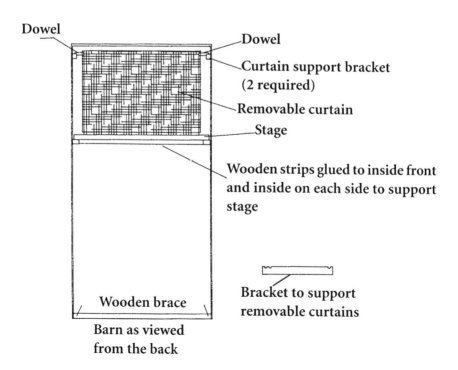

Stage

Removable
Curtain

Removable
Backdrop

Looking down into
the barn from above

Top removed
for easier viewing

Dowel

Dowel

Curtain support bracket
(2 required)

Removable curtain

Stage

Wooden strips glued to inside front
and inside on each side to support
stage

Wooden brace

Bracket to support
removable curtains

Barn as viewed
from the back

Small Version

The small version of the Old Barn Puppet Theater works well for stick puppet plays. It should measure about 24" from top to bottom, and 21" from the side to the silo. The sides of the barn may vary but should measure about 4 to 6" from the front to the back. Start by finding a cardboard box big enough to meet these dimensions.

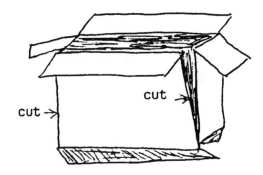

1. Remove one long side of the box, keeping the bottom and top flaps attached. This piece will be the basis for the barn. The flaps will be the sides of the theater and will support the roof.

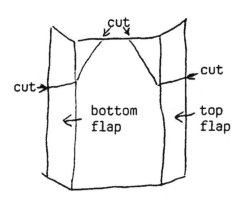

2. Turn this piece of cardboard on its side. Cut as shown. This forms a gable with two slanted sides and a flat top.

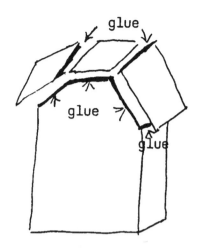

3. With the leftover cardboard cut two rectangles as wide as the slanted sides of the gable, and one as wide as the flat top. Glue to the top of the barn as shown. Hold in place with wide masking tape.

4. Glue black construction paper on the roof. Glue red construction paper on the front of the barn, covering the flaps, or sides.

5. Cut strips out of white construction paper. Glue to the front of the barn, to form a barn door.

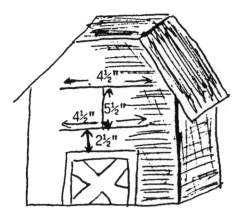

6. Measure up from the barn door 2½", and cut across 4½", then cut across the other way 4½". From the center of this cut, cut up 5½", then cut across the top the same way you did the bottom, 4½" both ways. This will form doors that open to reveal the stage area.

7. Bend the doors open. Put a piece of Velcro on the back of each door, and a corresponding piece on each edge of the roof, so the doors can be held open by pressing them against the Velcro on the roof. Color black X marks on the doors as shown.

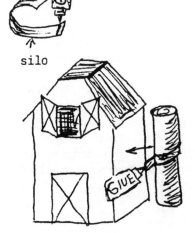

8. To make the silo, coil a piece of red construction paper and secure the edge with glue. Cut a red strip of paper and use it to glue the silo to the side of the barn.

9. Glue pieces of straw around the edge of the top of the silo. With the black construction paper cut a half circle, then form into a cone and glue edges together to make a roof. Glue roof onto silo.

velcro

velcro

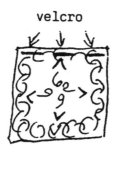

10. Glue a strip of Velcro inside the barn roof, along the top and sides. Glue the corresponding strip to the long edge of the bandanna. Secure in place. This is the backdrop.

11. For hayloft, cut two pieces of cardboard 6" long by 4" wide. Cut one more piece 6½" long by 5" wide and cut the top corners off. Glue the pieces together as shown. Hold in place with wide masking tape.

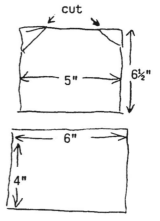

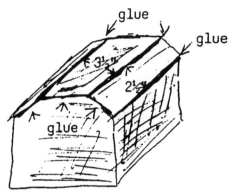

12. For the roof of the hay-loft, cut two pieces of cardboard 6½" long by 2½" wide. Cut a third piece 6½" long by 3½" wide. Glue them so that the 3½" piece is the middle of the roof. Hold in place with wide masking tape.

13. Cover the hayloft with red construction paper. Cover the roof with black construction paper. Cut a small square piece of black construction paper and glue to the front of the hayloft. Cut thin srips of white paper and glue in place to look like doors on the front of the hayloft. Glue hayloft to the top of the barn.

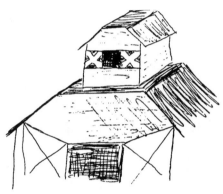

14. Finish by gluing straw onto the black square, so it looks like the hay is coming out of the loft. Draw, color, and cut out a rooster. Glue him to toothpicks. Make a crisscross with two toothpicks, and glue in the center. Make signs reading "N," "S," "E" and "W" and glue them to the ends of the toothpicks. This is the weathervane. If you want to be fancy, draw two cornstalks on yellow construction paper, cut them out and glue them to the front of your barn, beside the front barn doors.

Invitations

If you are planning a big production, it might be fun to issue written invitations. Draw a barn on red construction paper; cut doors so that they open. (See illustration.) Beneath the doors, insert a card telling the date, time and place of your production.

Sketch of invitation. Cut barn doors along dotted lines. Insert card with date, time, and place under doors so it shows when doors are opened.

How to Make
Old Barn Puppets

There are two kinds of Old Barn puppets: stick puppets and dowel puppets. To make a stick puppet, simply photocopy the desired picture from this book and color it. Cut it out, then lay the picture on firm, white cardboard and trace around it. Cut the shape from the cardboard. Glue one end of a tongue depressor near the bottom of the cardboard shape. Now glue the paper puppet to this cardboard backing, sandwiching the tongue depressor between the cardboard and paper layers. This completes your stick puppet.

Stick puppets work well on a small stage or behind the edge of a table. Remember when using stick puppets that the front of each puppet must face the audience at all times.

The dowel puppets are more like dolls. They have three-dimensional bodies and are supported on 12-inch dowel rods. These puppets take more time to make than stick puppets. You must take extra care to follow the directions and study the photographs of the puppets. Directions for Barnwell family dowel puppets begin on page 19. Directions for other dowel puppets follow the plays in which they appear, as do the pictures you will use for stick puppets.

If you prefer, you can substitute a stick puppet for any dowel puppet in this book. Simply photocopy the line drawing of the finished dowel puppet and make it into a stick puppet as described above. (You will probably want to add feet.)

Scarecrows is a stick puppet play, but Big Crow is a dowel puppet. For a stick puppet Big Crow, photocopy the drawing of the dowel puppet.

Gertie Goat is a stick puppet play.

Gone Fishing is a dowel puppet play. All the puppets are dowel puppets except the fish and Roly Worm.

Camping Out and **Who Stole the Pie?** are dowel puppet plays.

Froggie Woggies is a stick puppet play. These puppets are especially fun to color and decorate.

The Computer is a dowel puppet play.

Farmer Barnwell Dowel Puppet

Begin with a ½" wood dowel, about 12" long. Push dowel into a round or egg-shaped foam ball (about 2½" is a good size for the ball, which will be your puppet's head). You may wish to glue the ball onto the dowel to keep it secure.

Now make Farmer Barnwell's face by attaching eyes (they can be roly eyes from a craft store, or felt), nose and mouth (felt), and a mustache. Glue on some wig air or other artificial hair, and add a small straw hat. Cut a triangle of fabric from a bandanna or other cotton print. Tie around dowel under Farmer Barnwell's head to be a scarf. Glue in place. Now you can begin to dress the dowel.

All the clothing pieces are glued together inside out and then turned right side out when the glue dries. Photocopy or trace the clothing patterns and cut them out. Lay them on the fabric of your choice. (Denim is a good choice for the overalls. It is a nice touch to cut the bib from the waistband of a

Farmer Barnwell shirt
cut two

Farmer Barnwell
hand — cut 2 from felt

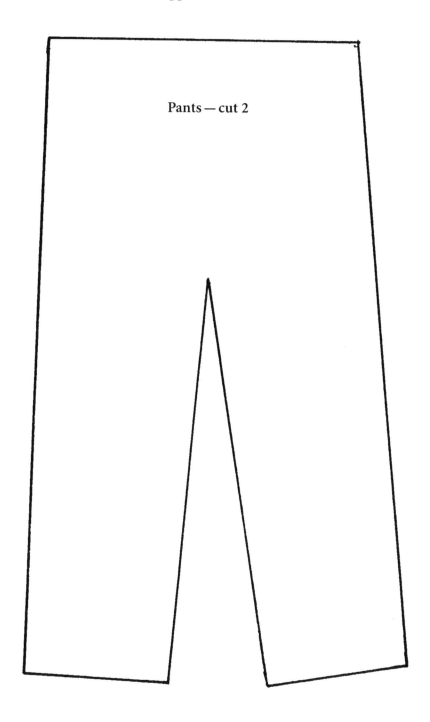

Pants — cut 2

Shoulder strap — cut 2

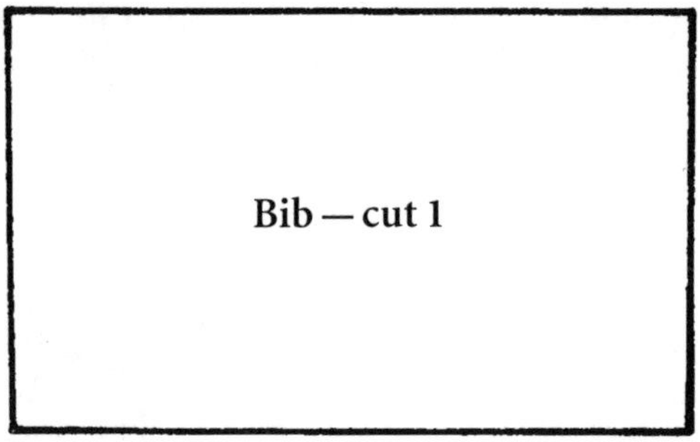

Bib — cut 1

Finished Farmer Barnwell dowel puppet

Farmer Barnwell dowel puppet

pair of jeans so that the stitching shows.) Cut out the fabric according to the pattern pieces, then assemble clothes as follows. Glue together at sides, under arms, and across top, leaving a small opening in center of top for neck. Turn right side out when glue dries. Cut 2 hands from felt. Glue hands into shirt sleeves. Set aside.

For the pants, glue the side seams together first (remember to glue then inside out), then the middle seam, leaving an opening for the dowel. Now glue the bib to the front of the pants. Bend two pieces of wire to look like buckles from a pair of suspenders. Pull the shoulder straps through the wire. Glue ends to front of bib and glue a small button over each.

Push a little stuffing into the sleeves of the shirt. Push an empty toilet paper tube into shirt. Push the dowel through the toilet paper tube and through the neck of the shirt. Glue shirt to the dowel stick under the scarf. Put the pants on, over the toilet paper tube, pushing the dowel through the hole. Tuck the shirt in. Glue the shoulder straps to the back of the pants.

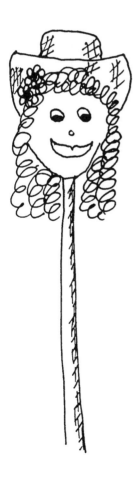

Rosie and Daisy Barnwell Dowel Puppets

Attach foam ball to dowel for head, as for Farmer Barnwell. Rosie and Daisy have curly hair and are wearing straw hats and a few flowers in their hair.

All of the clothing pieces are glued together inside out and then turned right side out when the glue dries. Use the pants pattern for Farmer Barnwell (page 21), omitting bib and straps and cutting the pants a little shorter (to represent a child's legs). Photocopy or trace the clothing patterns and cut them out. Lay them on the fabric of your choice. (Flowered material is good for the shirts, denim for the pants.) Cut out the fabric according to the pattern pieces, then assemble clothes as follows. Glue shirt together up the sides, under the arms, and across the top, leaving a small opening in center of top (fold line) for the dowel. Turn right side out. Push the dowel through and glue fabric to dowel around the neck. Glue

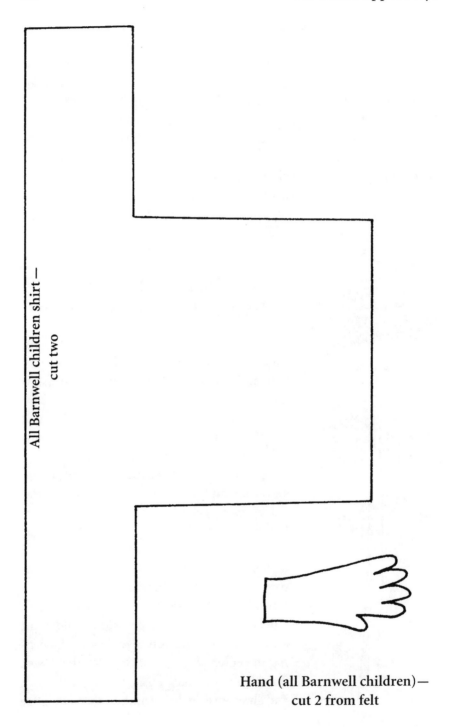

All Barnwell children shirt —
cut two

Hand (all Barnwell children)—
cut 2 from felt

Finished Rosie or Daisy Barnwell dowel puppet

the pants together, first the outer seams and then the middle seam, leaving an opening for the dowel. Put a toilet paper tube into shirt, along with stuffing in arms. Leave an opening in the back of the pants, for the dowel. Push the dowel through the top of the pants going over the toilet paper roll. Glue the toilet paper roll to the inside of the pants. Tuck the shirt in and wrap a piece of ribbon around her middle and glue in place. Cut two hands from felt and glue into shirt sleeves.

Bobby Barnwell Dowel Puppet

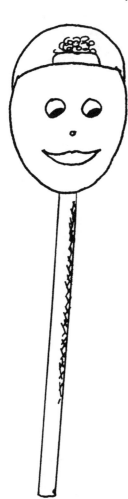

Attach foam ball to dowel for head, as for Farmer Barnwell. Attach eyes, nose and mouth; Bobby's hat and hair will be added after the body is made. Cut a scarf from the corner of a red bandanna and tie below head, gluing in place on dowel.

Photocopy shirt pattern for Barnwell children (page 26) and pants pattern for Farmer Barnwell (page 21), cutting pants legs a bit shorter (to represent a child's legs). Photocopy patterns on page 29 for Bobby's cap, brim, and shirt pocket. Use denim for pants, a plaid cotton for shirt and pocket, and red felt for cap. To assemble clothing and body, follow instructions for Rosie and Daisy Barnwell puppet. Add shirt pocket. Add a black ribbon around Bobby's middle for a belt. Add a scrap for a pocket handkerchief, if you like.

Bobby's baseball cap should be cut from red felt. Glue the points together in this order: 6 to 1, 2 to 1, 3 to 2, 4 to 3 and 5 to 4. Glue brim onto cap. Glue strap in back. Glue cap backwards to Bobby's head. Add a few curls of hair peeking through the hole in back of cap.

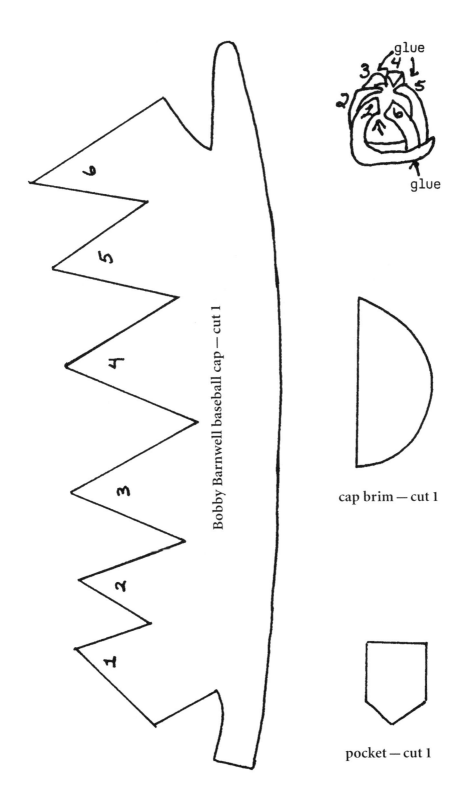

glue

3 4
glue
2 5
7 6

Bobby Barnwell baseball cap — cut 1

6

5

4

3

2

1

cap brim — cut 1

pocket — cut 1

Finished Bobby Barnwell dowel puppet

Bud Barnwell Dowel Puppet

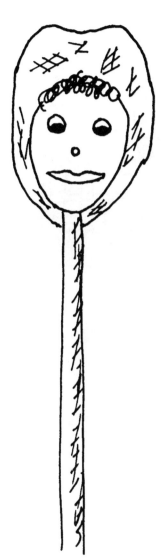

Attach foam ball to dowel for head, as for Farmer Barnwell. Bud has curly hair and wears a straw hat. Cut a scarf from the corner of a bandanna and tie below head, gluing in place on dowel.

Photocopy shirt pattern for Barnwell children (page 26) and pants pattern for Farmer Barnwell (page 21), as well as shirt pocket pattern for Bobby Barnwell (page 29). Use denim for pants and a lightweight fabric for shirt. To assemble clothing and body, follow instructions for Rosie and Daisy Barnwell puppet. Add shirt pocket. Add a black ribbon around Bud's middle for a belt. Add a scrap for a pocket handkerchief, if you like.

The Barnwell children (left to right): Bobby, the twins, and Bud.

Finished Bud Barnwell dowel puppet

Martha Barnwell Dowel Puppet

Begin as for Farmer Barnwell. Martha needs a generous hairdo (your color choice). Add some glasses, which you can make from any thin wire.

Photocopy the patterns for Martha's dress and smock and cut them out. Lay patterns on fabric of your choice (flowered material is good for dress). Be careful to observe fold lines. Cut according to pattern. For apron, cut a rectangle of white fabric 3½" × 11½" and another measuring 1½" × 6½". For hands, use Farmer Barnwell hand pattern and cut 2 from felt. Assemble as follows.

The dress is glued together inside out and then turned right side out when the glue dries. Glue the two dress pieces up the sides and under the arms, then along the top, leaving an opening at the neck for the dowel. Turn right side out. Put smock over the dress, pulling the arms through; glue smock in the back. Push the dowel through the neck opening and glue fabric to dowel at neck. For apron, the smaller of your two white rectangles is the band; the larger is the apron skirt. Glue apron skirt to one edge of band, making it ruffle as you go. Fold band in half over the edge of the apron that you just ruffled. (See illustration, page 36.) Put apron around Martha's middle and glue in the back. Cut hands from felt and glue into sleeve openings. Push a little bit of stuffing into arms. Put an empty toilet paper roll under dress so that the dowel goes through it, and glue in the back to the dowel. (See illustration, page 36.) Glue a piece of lace around the neck, making it ruffle just a little as you go. Glue in the back, gluing to the back of dress at the same time.

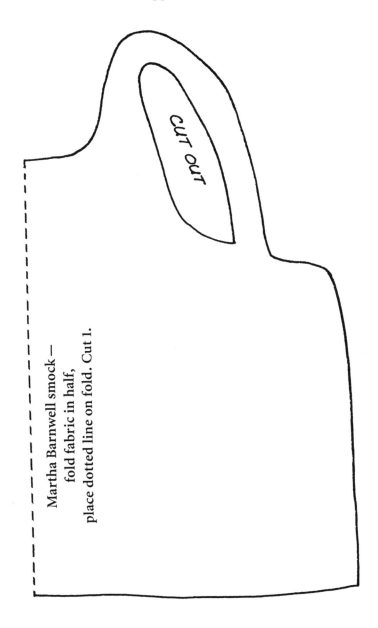

CUT OUT

Martha Barnwell smock —
fold fabric in half,
place dotted line on fold. Cut 1.

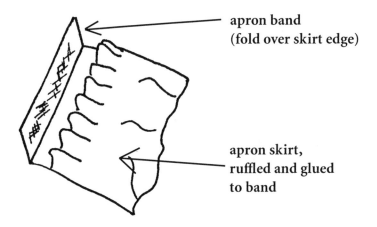

apron band
(fold over skirt edge)

apron skirt,
ruffled and glued
to band

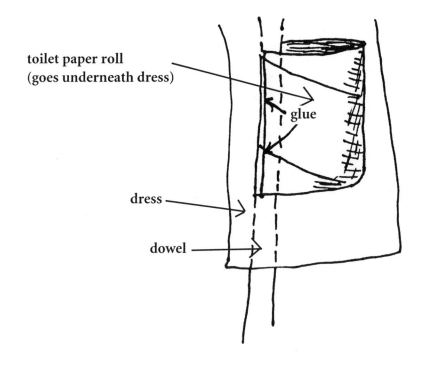

toilet paper roll
(goes underneath dress)

glue

dress

dowel

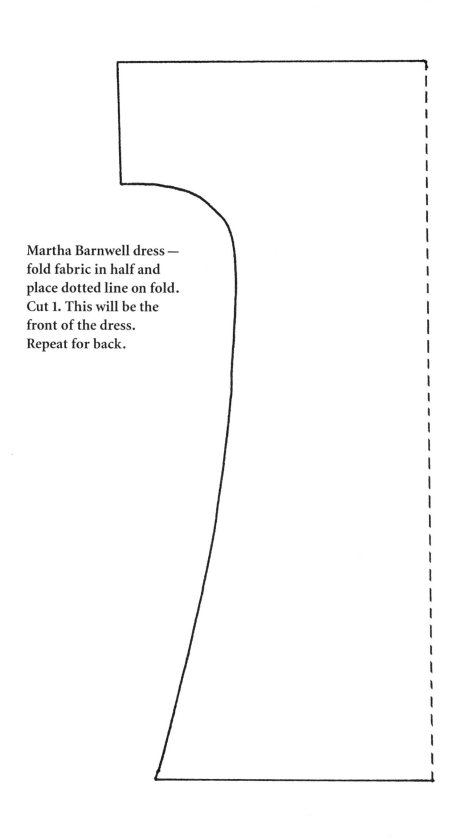

Martha Barnwell dress —
fold fabric in half and
place dotted line on fold.
Cut 1. This will be the
front of the dress.
Repeat for back.

Finished Martha Barnwell dowel puppet

Grandma Barnwell Dowel Puppet

Attach foam ball to dowel for head, as for Farmer Barnwell. Grandma has curly white hair and glasses (the glasses are easy to make from thin wire).

Photocopy pattern for Martha Barnwell's dress (excluding smock and apron) and hands and follow instructions for cutting and assembling. When dress is assembled and glued to the dowel at neck, push a little bit of stuffing up the back of the dress, just enough to make Grandma look a little hunched over. Put an empty toilet paper roll inside the dress and glue to the dowel, making sure the dowel goes into the middle of the roll. This will hold the stuffing in place. Wrap a piece of pink ribbon around Grandma's

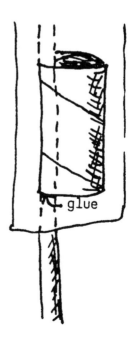

Finished Grandma Barnwell dowel puppet

middle, and glue in place. Cut a piece of the kind of craft ribbon that is manufactured with a wire in it. Wrinkle it around Grandma's neck so that it ruffles just a little, and glue in the back. Cut a 6" piece of pearls on a string. Put around Grandma's neck and glue in the back.

The cast of *Scarecrows*, with dowel puppet Farmer Barnwell and crows. Stick puppets may also be used.

Scarecrows

WHERE: Farmer Barnwell's cornfield. WHEN: Summer. PUPPETS: Six speaking characters, plus any number of crows. TIME: Approximately 10 minutes.

CHARACTERS

FARMER BARNWELL. . . Owner of the Barnwell Farm
SCAT . . . . Farmer Barnwell's scarecrow
SHOO FLY . . . . Scat's scarecrow friend
BOO . . . . Another scarecrow friend
GIT . . . . Another scarecrow friend
BIG CROW . . . . Boss of the other crows
OTHER CROWS . . . . . As many as desired

At Rise: A blue sky backdrop is dotted with white clouds. Upright rows of green leaves with corn husks are taped to front edge of stage to represent growing corn. Crows are flying around the stage. Farmer Barnwell speaks to Scat in a loud voice.

FARMER BARNWELL: Scat Scarecrow, what's your problem here? Look at all those pesky crows in my cornfield. They are eating up my good corn. Why aren't you chasing them away? That's your job, you know.

SCAT: I know, Farmer Barnwell, but I can't make the crows leave your corn alone this year. I think it is because your corn is the sweetest and tenderest it has ever been, and the crows love it.

FARMER BARNWELL: That's all the more reason you should be protecting my corn. Start shooing and scaring them away.

43

SCAT: I will do my best, Farmer Barnwell.

FARMER BARNWELL: You'd better, or I will find someone who can do the job. *(Exits.)*

(CROWS fly around stage, cawing and teasing Scat.)

SCAT: What am I to do? I shoo and boo until I am out of breath. Shoo! Boo! Scat, you old crow! Darn these crows! They just laugh and crow back at me.

(CROWS keep flying around stage, laughing and cawing.)

SCAT: *(Runs after crows.)* Away with you! Go to someone else's cornfield. Leave Farmer Barnwell's cornfield alone! Shoooooooo! Do you hear me, you corn-eating crows?

(CROWS fly around the stage cawing loudly.)

SCAT: *(Sighs.)* It's no use. I have lost my scaring power. I can't make them leave. But if they don't leave, I will lose my job as Farmer Barnwell's scarecrow! I have been his scarecrow for many years. This is a sad day for me. *(Walks back and forth on the stage muttering to himself.)* I'll no longer be a crow-scarer. Oh, I feel so bad.

(CROWS keep flying around the stage.)

FARMER BARNWELL: *(Enters.)* Scat! You have not scared away one crow.

SCAT: I know, and I've tried. I've really tried.

FARMER BARNWELL: You'd better get rid of those crows before I get back again, or ...

SCAT: I'm out of the scarecrow business.

FARMER BARNWELL: Right. *(Exits.)*

(CROWS fly around the stage, cawing loudly.)

SCAT: I need help. What can I do?

(CROWS fly close to Scat, cawing loudly. BIG CROW lands on Scat's head.)

BIG CROW: Scat Scarecrow, you have shooed us out of Farmer Barnwell's cornfield for the last time. Caw! Caw! Caw!

SCAT: Think you're big, don't you, Big Crow?

BIG CROW: I am big. I am the biggest crow around. I am Boss Crow. I call the shots. My friends and I are taking over Farmer Barnwell's cornfield. We like his new, sweet and tender corn, and no other farmer's corn can compare. So there! Caw! Caw!

FARMER BARNWELL: *(Enters.)* Scat Scarecrow! *(Walks around.)* You are a bum crow-scarer. I'm sorry, but you are fired! *(Exits.)*

(Offstage voices are heard, crying, "Shoo! Boo! Git! Fly away!" The words become a chant as SHOO FLY, BOO, *and* GIT *enter. The chant grows louder and louder. The scarecrows have tin pans in their hands. They swing around and hit each other's pans, making a tremendous noise. [The noise comes from backstage by someone hitting a real pie tin.])*

BIG CROW: Awwwwwwk! Farmer Barnwell must have hired professional crow-scarers! We're out of here on the wing!

(CROWS *fly away, cawing.*)

SCAT: This is awesome! My scarecrow friends have come to help me. The crows have gone.

(SCARECROW FRIENDS *stop the banging noise.*)

SCAT: Thank you, Shoo Fly, for shooing away the crows.

SHOO FLY: That's o.k., Scat. *(Exits.)*

SCAT: Thank you, Boo, for booing away the crows.

BOO: Happy to help out. *(Exits.)*

SCAT: Thanks, Git, for telling those old crows to git.

GIT: Any time. You'd do the same for us. What are friends for? *(Exits.)*

SCAT: When you can't do something alone, and you don't know what to do, there is nothing better than having good friends to help you. (SCAT *shouts.*) Will you hang around until the new, sweet corn is picked and help me keep the crows away?

SCARECROW FRIENDS *(off stage)*: That we will.

(CROWS *return, flying around the stage and cawing. The* SCARECROW FRIENDS *(off stage) start up the chant and hang the pie tins. The crows fly away.*)

FARMER BARNWELL: *(Enters.)* That's the way to go, Scat. You've done a fine job. The crows are gone from my cornfield. I am proud of you. Good work!

SCAT: Thanks, Farmer Barnwell. I needed a little help from my friends.

FARMER BARNWELL: Friends?

SCAT: Yes, my friends are standing by to help me shoo away the crows until the corn is picked.

FARMER BARNWELL: Well, I'll be. Your friends have come to the rescue. There's nothing like friends. Where are they?

SCAT: *(Calls.)* Come out, Boo.

(Boo *enters.*)

Scat: This is Boo. Come out, Shoo Fly.

(Shoo Fly *enters.*)

Scat: This is Shoo Fly. Come out, Git.

(Git *enters.*)

Scat: This is Git.

Farmer Barnwell: I'm glad to meet Scat's good friends. Thank you for lending Scat a hand.

Scat: And saving my job!

(Crows *fly around stage, cawing.* Scarecrows *beat the pie tins and shout.* Crows *fly away.*)

Farmer Barnwell: With you scarecrows on the job, and Scat as your leader, we'll have good sweet corn this year after all. Oh, happy summer's day!

Curtain.

Props: Pie tins or other pans for banging backstage.

Production notes: Blue burlap makes a good sky backdrop, and white felt is good for clouds.

How to Make Scarecrow Puppets

These stick puppets are made of cardboard, felt, and fabrics of your choice. Photocopy the scarecrow and clothing patterns on pages 48 and 49. Cut out the photocopied patterns. Lay them on sturdy cardboard and trace around them. Cut them out. Now lay the cardboard patterns on the fabric you have chosen for the scarecrows and their clothes. (Felt works best for the bodies; clothing can be felt in different colors, or scraps of other fabrics.) Trace around them and cut out the scarecrow shapes. Glue a tongue depressor to each cardboard shape, then glue scarecrow shape to cardboard over the tongue depressor. Now cut out the clothing shapes and glue them to the scarecrow bodies. Glue on straw for hair. Buttons are a nice touch for the clothes; you can also use them for eyes, or use roly eyes (available in craft stores). Glue small squares of fabric onto clothing to look like patches. When you have finished decorating your scarecrow puppets, glue a tongue depressor to the back of each one.

To make pie tins for scarecrows to hold, cut a small circle from an index card. Take a two-inch square of aluminum foil and fold over the circle. Crimp foil so edges stand up around the circle, resembling the edge of a pie tin. Cut away any pieces of the aluminum foil that stand up too much. Attach with sticky-on-both-sides tape to the three scarecrow friends' right arms.

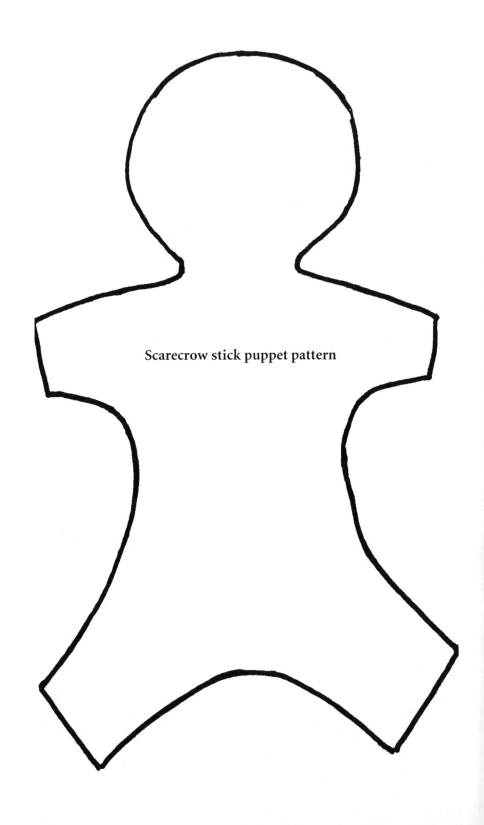

Scarecrow stick puppet pattern

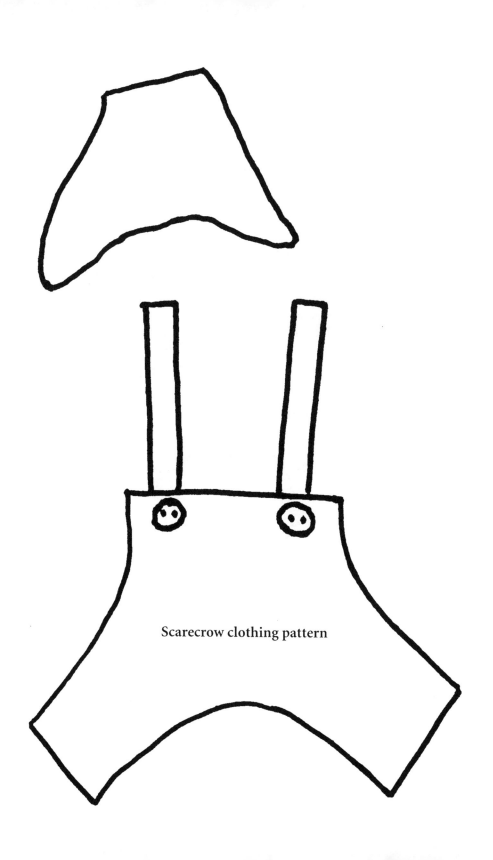

Scarecrow clothing pattern

How to Make a Crow

For Big Crow, begin with a 1½" foam ball (for the head) and a 3" foam ball (for the body). Smaller balls can be used for other crows. Glue the 1½" ball on an angle to the 3" ball. (It is easier to glue them together if you cut a thin slice off each ball to give you a flat gluing surface.) Insert a dowel stick into the larger ball. (See illustration.)

Photocopy the patterns for the wings and the tail and cut them out. Use them to cut wings, body and tail from black felt. Glue each two wing pieces together, leaving flat ends open; don't turn inside out. Glue wings to body. Glue the two tail pieces together and glue them to body. Cover the rest of the crow with black felt, covering head. Cut two beak pieces from yellow felt, glue together, and glue to front of crow's face. Glue on roly eyes.

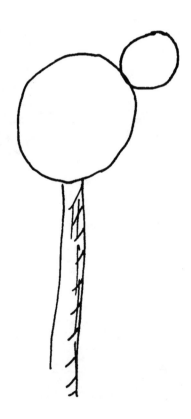

glue

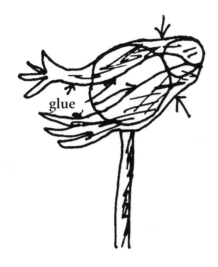

glue

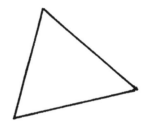

**Big Crow beak —
Cut 2**

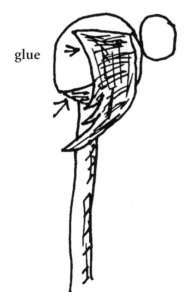

glue

smaller crow beak —
cut 2

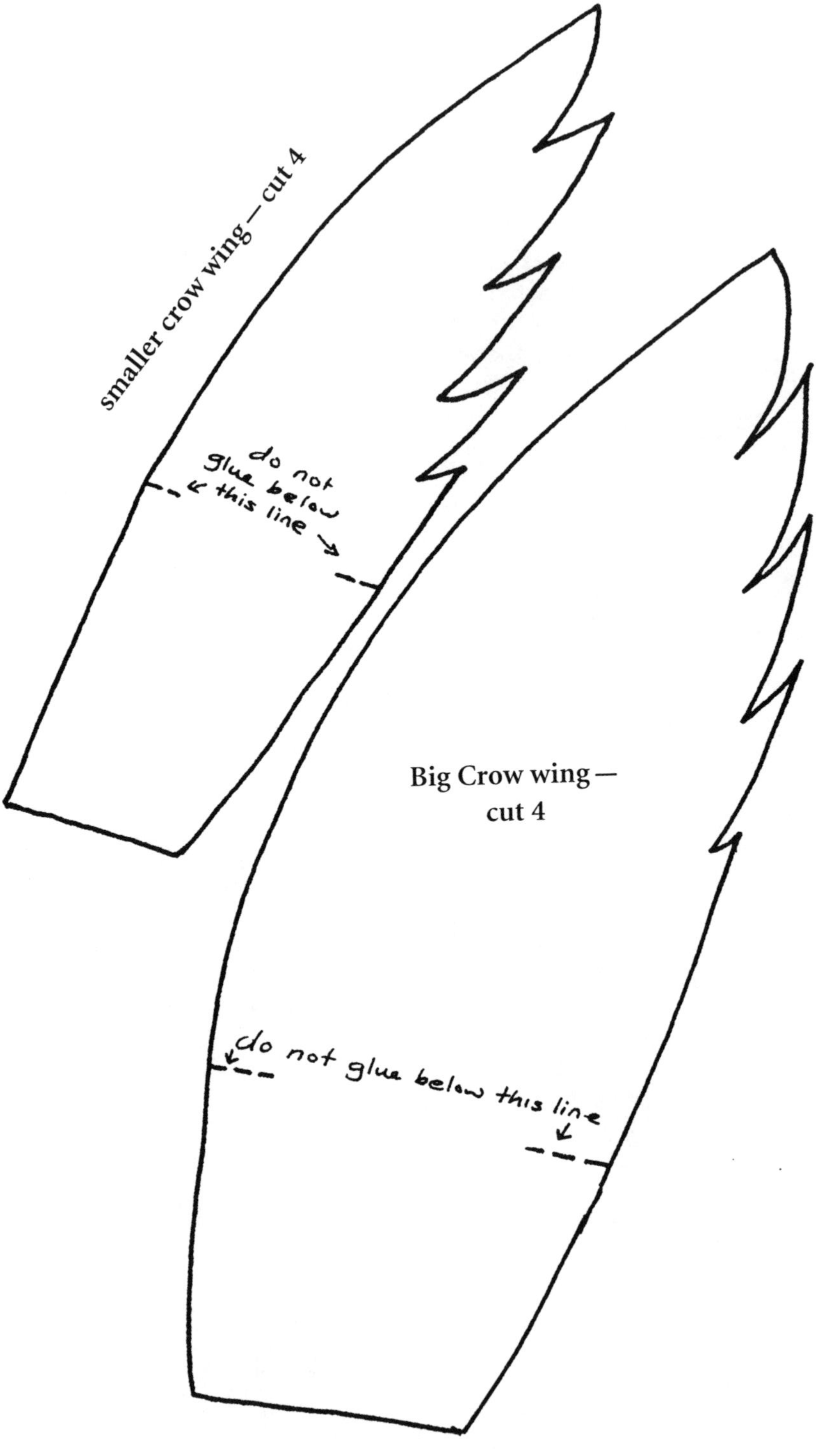

smaller crow wing — cut 4

do not glue below this line →

Big Crow wing —
cut 4

do not glue below this line ↓

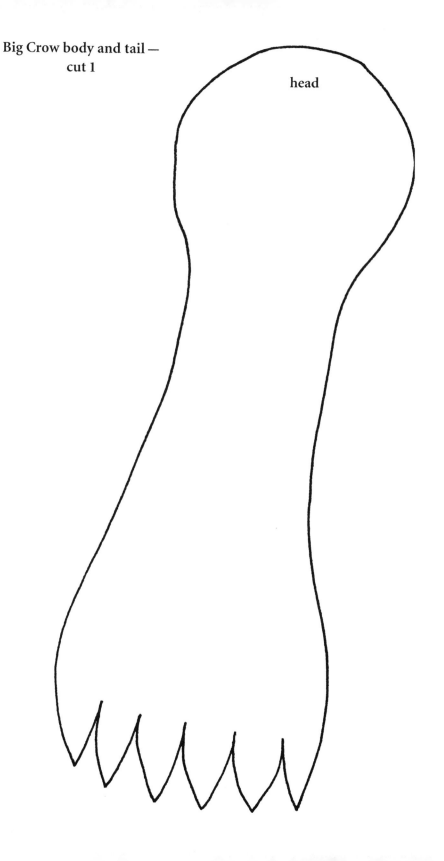

Big Crow body and tail —
cut 1

head

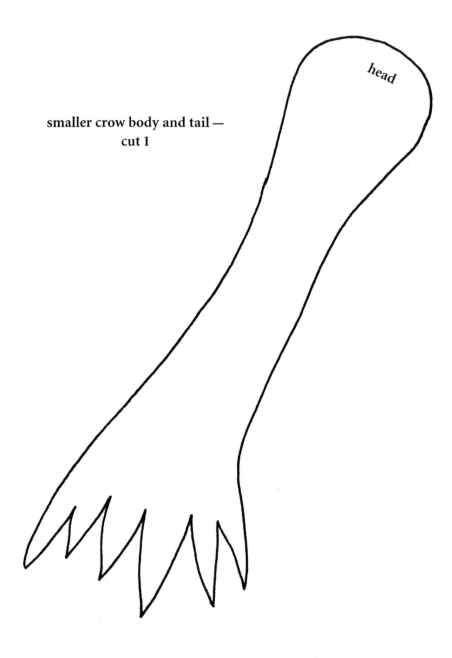

smaller crow body and tail —
cut 1

head

Finished Crow dowel puppet

Talkabout

1. Why do farmers put up scarecrows?
     (To scare away the crows.)
2. Why do farmers want to scare away the crows?
     (Because the crows eat up all the corn.)
3. Where do farmers put the scarecrows?
     (In the ground in the cornfield.)
4. Have you ever seen a real scarecrow in a cornfield?
5. Where did you see the scarecrow?
6. How would you make a scarecrow?
     (With hay, straw, etc.)
7. Why do the crows like Farmer Barnwell's corn to eat better than the other farmers' corn?
     (Farmer Barnwell grows the sweetest corn of all the farmers.)
8. When does Farmer Barnwell put out his scarecrow?
     (In the spring when the corn is planted and the green sprouts come up out of the ground.)
9. When do you eat corn?
     (In the late summer when the kernels are ripe.)
10. Why do farmers grow corn?
     (To sell some, to have some for their family, feed the pigs, give to neighbors whose crop didn't do well because of corn bugs, corn disease or crows.)
11. How many food products can you name that are made with corn?
     (Popcorn, cornflakes, corn muffins, corn syrup, corn bread...)
12. Did you know that Christopher Columbus found Indians growing corn when he came to America? What year did Columbus come to America?
     (1492)
13. Do you know what a corny story is?
14. Does anyone here know a short corny story?

Gertie Goat

WHERE: Farmer Barnwell's meadow.   WHEN: Summer.   PUPPETS: Three speaking characters, plus train.   TIME: Approximately 10 minutes.

CHARACTERS

FARMER BARNWELL. . . Owner of the Barnwell Farm
MARTHA BARNWELL . . His wife
GERTIE GOAT. . . . . . Barnwell's naughty goat

At Rise: A blue sky backdrop is dotted with white clouds. Farmer Barnwell is standing center stage.

———————————

FARMER BARNWELL: *(Loudly.)* Gertie Goat! Come here!

GERTIE GOAT: *(Offstage.)* Baaaaaaaaaaa.

FARMER BARNWELL: Gertie Goat! Do you hear me? Come here!

GERTIE GOAT: *(Enters.)* Baaaaaaaa. *(Goes to Farmer Barnwell. She has blue denim fabric in her mouth.)*

FARMER BARNWELL: What have you been chewing on today? *(Leans towards Gertie Goat.)*

GERTIE GOAT: Baaaaaaaa.

FARMER BARNWELL: *(Shouts.)* Gertie Goat! You are chewing on my brand new blue jeans. I just bought those jeans!

GERTIE GOAT: Baaaaaaa. *(Jumps up and down.)*

FARMER BARNWELL: Those jeans are the only ones I ever found that fit me right.

*(*GERTIE GOAT *jumps up and down.)*

57

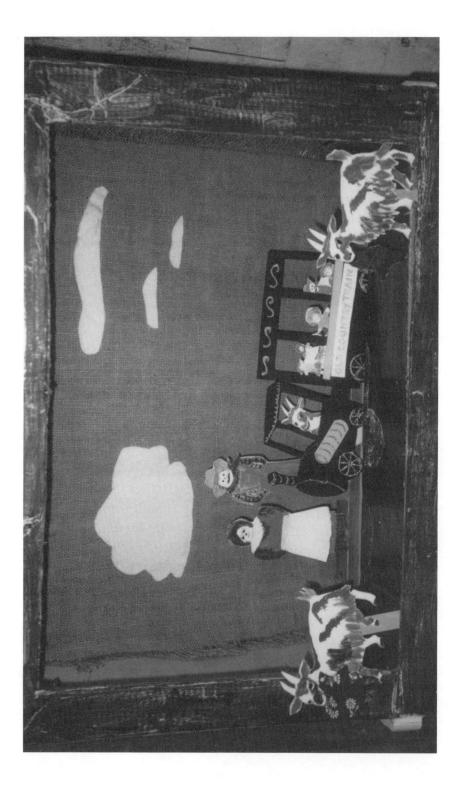

FARMER BARNWELL: They cost me a pretty penny.

GERTIE GOAT: Baaaaaaaa. *(Jumps up and down.)*

FARMER BARNWELL: And I was going to wear them to the barn dance on Saturday night.

GERTIE GOAT: *(Dances around and sings.)* Baa, baa, baa!

FARMER BARNWELL: You are a naughty goat! A very naughty goat!

GERTIE GOAT: *(Sadly.)* Baaaaaaaaa.

FARMER BARNWELL: Get along with you. I have work to do. No more chewing up people's clothes. Do you hear me?

GERTIE GOAT: Baa. *(Exits.)*

MARTHA BARNWELL: *(Calling from offstage.)* Harry! Oh, Harry!

FARMER BARNWELL: I'm here in the meadow, Martha.

MARTHA BARNWELL: *(Enters.)* Oh, Harry. The strangest thing has happened. I can't find my best dress.

FARMER BARNWELL: Which is your best dress?

MARTHA BARNWELL: *(Crossly.)* You know, the red one!

FARMER BARNWELL: Which red one?

MARTHA BARNWELL: The one I'm not wearing! It's my best dress, and I can't find it.

FARMER BARNWELL: Where did you have it last?

MARTHA BARNWELL: It was hanging in my closet. I went to iron it for my church meeting tonight, and it was gone!

FARMER BARNWELL: You will have to find it yourself. I am late with my chores. That drat Gertie Goat took up so much of my time. *(Exits.)*

MARTHA BARNWELL: A great help you are! *(Starts to exit.)*

GERTIE GOAT: *(Enters. She has red fabric in mouth.)* Baaaaaaaa.

MARTHA BARNWELL: *(Screams.)* Gertie Goat! *(They bump together. They pull apart.)* Gertie Goat, what do you have in your mouth?

(GERTIE GOAT starts to back away.)

MARTHA BARNWELL: Come to me this minute!

GERTIE GOAT: Baaaaaa. *(Moves one jump towards Martha.)*

MARTHA BARNWELL: *(Shouts.)* Come here!

GERTIE GOAT: *(Jumps fast to Martha.)* Baaaa! Baaaaa!

MARTHA BARNWELL: *(Leans towards GERTIE GOAT and screams*

Opposite: Stick-puppet cast of *Gertie Goat* (note the use of two Gertie puppets with different fabric in mouths).

loudly.) My dress! My red dress! My best red dress! You have chewed up my best Sunday-go-to-meeting dress. Oh, you naughty, naughty, naughty goat! Oh! You miserable, no-good, clothes-eating goat!

GERTIE GOAT: *(Sadly.)* Baaaaaaaa.

MARTHA BARNWELL: I could cry!

GERTIE GOAT: *(Jumps up and down.)* Baaaaa. Baaaaa.

MARTHA BARNWELL: I think I will cry.

GERTIE GOAT: *(Jumps up and down.)* Baaaaa. Baaaaa. *(Exits.)*

(MARTHA BARNWELL cries up a storm, then exits.)

FARMER BARNWELL: *(Enters.)* My next job is to mow the field. Work! Work! Work!

GERTIE GOAT: *(Enters. Has straw material or hat in mouth. Jumps around.)* Baaaaaaaaa.

FARMER BARNWELL: Come here, Gertie Goat. What are you chewing on now? You are chewing on my *favorite* fishing hat! My *favorite, favorite,* most precious and *old* fishing hat! No other hat will do. That does it! I can never forgive you. *(Shakes head.)*

GERTIE GOAT: *(Sadly.)* Baa. Baa. Baa.

FARMER BARNWELL: Gertie Goat. I am sorry to tell you this, but we can't afford to have you around any more. Today you chewed up my wife's best red dress. You chewed up my new jeans, and now you chewed up my favorite old fishing hat. Yesterday, you chewed up the children's sneakers, and the day before that, my wife's Sunday lace tablecloth. We can't keep you on the farm any more. We can't afford it.

GERTIE GOAT: *(Sadly.)* Baaaaaaaa.

FARMER BARNWELL: You'll have to leave and find a job. You'll have to take care of yourself. I'm sorry, but that's the way it is.

GERTIE GOAT: *(Sadly.)* Baaaaa. *(Exits.)*

FARMER BARNWELL: I hate to make Gertie Goat leave, but there is no other way. If I was a rich farmer, it would be different. Poor Gertie! Out in the big, cruel world all by herself. We will miss her. This is a sad day for us all on the Barnwell Farm.

Curtain.

SCENE 2

(Curtain opens on the same setting. It is one week later.)

FARMER BARNWELL: I'm glad I got the field plowed, fixed the water pump, and cleaned out the chicken coop. Everything's going great, except we miss old Gertie Goat.

(Train whistle heard offstage.)

FARMER BARNWELL: Can that be? Am I hearing the whistle on the Old Country Train? It hasn't been running for five years! It always used to toot through our meadow two times a day, all summer long. Then nobody wanted to bother with it. It stood out in the sun and rain until it rusted.

(Train whistle blows again, only louder.)

FARMER BARNWELL: Jumping haystacks! That *is* the Old Country Train's whistle! There is no other whistle like that in the whole world!

(Chug-chug sounds offstage. Train whistle blows very loudly.)

FARMER BARNWELL: *(Very excited.)* Here she comes! Here comes the Old Country Train, and it's full of passengers!

(Train enters and crosses the stage.)

FARMER BARNWELL: *(Jumps up and down and shouts.)* Jumping haystacks! I can't believe my eyes! Look who is the engineer of the Old Country Train! It's Gertie Goat! Our Gertie Goat! Hi, Gertie! *(Jumps up and down. Runs after the train, shouting.)*

(Train whistle blows.)

FARMER BARNWELL: *(Yells.)* Hey, Gertie, I always said you were a smart goat. Now you are the engineer for the Old Country Train. What a great job! What a great goat! What a great thing to do, to make so many children happy! Now you can afford to buy your own shoes, dresses and fishing hats to chew up! You can come back and live on the farm! We miss you! *(He follows the train, yelling.)* We want you home! *(Train moves slowly across the stage.)*

GERTIE GOAT: Baaaaaaaaa. Soon you will have three pairs of jeans in different colors and a sportsman's fishing hat for you to make up for the ones I chewed up.

FARMER BARNWELL: *(Jumps up and down.)* Hot diggity dog!

GERTIE GOAT: And Mom Barnwell, soon you can buy a new dress for every holiday of the year.

MARTHA BARNWELL: Oh, my! Oh, my word! Thank you, Gertie.

GERTIE GOAT: And tell the kids that soon they can have a pair of high stepping sneakers! See you soon!

(Train whistle blows. Train keeps moving across stage.)

FARMER BARNWELL: Come home, Gertie. We miss you.

GERTIE GOAT: *(Loudly.)* I miss you, too.
(Train whistle blows loudly three times. Train exits.)
FARMER BARNWELL: *(Shouts.)* I hope we will be seeing you, Gertie.
(Train gives three big whistles.)
FARMER BARNWELL: Hot diggity dog! See you soon, you old goat!
Curtain.

Props: Blue jean material, red material, straw material or small straw hat; train whistle.

For Farmer Barnwell and Martha Barnwell, photocopy drawings on pages 63 and 64. Use these drawings for stick puppets.

Production notes: You can attach the different fabrics to Gertie Goat's mouth using Velcro, or make three different Gertie Goat puppets with a different scrap of fabric glued to each one's mouth.

How to Make
"Gertie Goat" Stick Puppets

For Gertie, simply photocopy the picture on page 66 and cut it out. Lay the cut-out picture on sturdy cardboard and trace around it. Cut the shape out of cardboard and glue it to one end of a tongue depressor. Glue paper puppet to cardboard so that tongue depressor is sandwiched between the layers. Follow the same principle for making Farmer Barnwell and Martha Barnwell.

For the old country train, photocopy the picture on page 65. Color the picture (coloring the train black will give you the most authentic look.) Cut out the picture. Cut out the areas around Gertie and the passengers so they will appear to be looking out from windows. (If this is too difficult, try coloring the spaces blue to suggest the sky.) Glue a cardboard backing to train, sandwiching two tongue depressors between the train and the backing. (The tongue depressors will move the train across the stage as a stick puppet.)

Finished Farmer Barnwell stick puppet

Finished Martha Barnwell stick puppet

Finished Old Country Train stick puppet

Gertie Goat stick puppet

Talkabout

1. Have you ever seen a real live goat? Where? When?
2. Goats like to chew on most anything. What things belonging to the Barnwells did Gertie Goat chew to pieces?

    (Farmer Barnwell's favorite jeans and his special fishing hat. Martha Barnwell's new red dress and her lace tablecloth. The children's sneakers.)
3. What's a female goat called?

    (A nanny goat or a doe.)
4. What's a billy goat?

    (A male goat.)
5. What's another name for a male goat?

    (A buck.)

6. What's a baby goat called?
   (A kid.)
7. Have you ever drunk goat's milk?
8. If you have, did you like it?
   (Tell children that goat's milk is very healthy and people drink it all over the world.)
9. Why do you think goats can run and climb steep rocky hills so fast and easily?
   (Goats have small, pointed, split hooves so they won't slip or fall.)
10. A nanny goat has two or sometimes three kids a year. How many kids are in your family?
11. What do goats like to eat (besides Farmer Barnwell's clothes)?
   (Hay and grain.)
12. How do goats protect themselves?
   (They butt with their heads.)
13. Do you think Gertie Goat ever butted any of the Barnwell family?
   (Emphasize that Gertie was their pet goat and they all were family and loved each other.)
14. Then why did Gertie have to leave?
   (Farmer Barnwell couldn't afford to keep her because she chewed up their clothes.)
15. How did Gertie Goat make it right with Farmer Barnwell?
   (She got a job and planned to pay him back.)
16. What was her job?
   (Gertie was the engineer on the Old Country Train.)
17. Do you think Gertie went back to live with the Barnwells?

The cast of *Gone Fishing.*

Gone Fishing

WHERE: Fish Lake near the Barnwell Farm. WHEN: Summer.
PUPPETS: Four. A voice actor is needed to speak the lines of Roly Worm,
but Roly is not an independently operated puppet. TIME: Approximately 10 minutes.

CHARACTERS

FARMER BARNWELL. . . Owner of the old Barnwell Farm
MARTHA BARNWELL . . His wife
GRANDMA BARNWELL . Grandma of the Barnwell
                                  Family
GRIZZLY . . . . A big, black, fierce bear
ROLY WORM . . . . . . The worm on Farmer Barnwell's
                                  fishing line

At Rise: A blue sky backdrop is dotted with white clouds. Farmer Barnwell stands to one side of stage. He holds a fishing pole. Fishing line hangs offstage as if in the water. Roly Worm is on the end of Farmer Barnwell's line, but he cannot be seen at this point.

FARMER BARNWELL: Hey! Hey! Hey! I am Farmer Harry Barnwell. I am fishing at Fish Lake. Yesterday, I caught six nice fish. I hope I catch six nice fish today. I'm hungry for a fish dinner.
   (His fishing line is jerked from below stage.)
FARMER BARNWELL: *(Yells.)* I've got a nibble! *(Farmer Barnwell turns, and his line is tossed over front of stage. Roly Worm is on the fishing line.)* Drat! It's only you, Roly Worm. *(The line is swung back offstage as*

69

if thrown back in the water. Farmer Barnwell sings.) Catch a fish. Catch a fish. I'll catch six fish today.

> *(Fishing line is jerked.)*

FARMER BARNWELL: Hooray! I've got a biggy on my line this time. *(Fishing line is raised again. Roly Worm is still on it.)*

FARMER BARNWELL: Horsefeathers! No fish! Stop smiling, Roly Worm, you'll get yours. *(Line is put back offstage as if into the water.)* I'm disgusted. I haven't caught a fish yet.

MARTHA BARNWELL: *(Enters from opposite side, holding a fishing line, which also drags in the "water.")* What did you say, Harry? *(She stops on her side of stage.)*

FARMER BARNWELL: I haven't caught a fish yet. *(Shakes head.)*

MARTHA BARNWELL: I can't believe that. Not you, Harry!

FARMER BARNWELL: *(Sighs.)* Yes, me. Why are you fishing, Martha? You'd rather be baking.

MARTHA BARNWELL: I was hungry for a big fish dinner tonight, so I thought I'd try my luck. Just in case you're not lucky today.

FARMER BARNWELL: I'm always lucky fishing, you know that.

> *(MARTHA's fishing line is jerked from below stage.)*

MARTHA BARNWELL: *(Screams.)* Oh! Oh! Harry! I've got a bite! Oh! I've got a fish! I've got a fish! What do I do, Harry?

FARMER BARNWELL: *(Goes to Martha and is very excited.)* Set the hook! Set the hook!

MARTHA BARNWELL: How do I do that?

FARMER BARNWELL: Give your line a quick jerk!

MARTHA BARNWELL: Like this? *(Jerks her line over the front of stage. There is a nice-sized*
fish on it.)* Whoop-dee-dee! I caught a nice fish for dinner. *(Exits.)*

FARMER BARNWELL: Can you beat that? Of all the luck! I'll try her fishing spot. *(He moves to opposite side, dragging his line.)*

GRANDMA BARNWELL: *(Enters from other side, holding a pole and dragging the line in the "water.")* Hello, how's my favorite boy? How's the fishing?

FARMER BARNWELL: I'm fine, Grandma, but the fishing is not so good today.

GRANDMA BARNWELL: That's the way it goes some days. Remember, as I have always told you, you can't win 'em all. Take fishing as it comes. Take life as it comes.

Farmer Barnwell: You're quite a gal, Grandma.

Grandma Barnwell: Thank you, Son.

(Grandma's *fishing line is jerked very hard.*)

Grandma Barnwell: Whoop-dee-do! I've got a big one hooked. *(She pulls up a bigger fish than Martha's.)*

Farmer Barnwell: *(Very excited.)* You sure caught a big fish, Grandma! *(He walks to Grandma.)*

Grandma Barnwell: Sure did, my boy. There will be a fish dinner at the Barnwells' tonight. *(Exits dragging her fish.)*

Farmer Barnwell: Of all the luck! I'll take Grandma Barnwell's fishing spot and see if I am as lucky as she was. *(Goes to other side and fishes.)* Drat! I've never had such a bad day fishing. Never in all the years I've been fishing.

Grizzly: *(Enters on opposite side. He, too, has a fishing pole and drags line in "water.")* Grrrrr! *(He does not notice Farmer Barnwell, but stops and "fishes.")*

Farmer Barnwell: Jumping catfish! Old Grizzly is here. I hope he doesn't see me. Wouldn't you know, he's going fishing. Grizzly can be a mean old bear at any time. Never get a grizzly bear mad at you.

(Grizzly's *fishing line is jerked very hard. With a lot of grunting and pulling, Grizzly pulls up the biggest fish of all.*)

Farmer Barnwell: Wow! Holy mackerel! What a fish! That's the biggest fish ever caught at Fish Lake.

Grizzly: *(Starts to exit with his big fish.)*

Farmer Barnwell: Oh, Mr. G-G-G-Grizzly, wait up! Please! I want to ask you something. I was wondering ... C-C-C-Could I ...

Grizzly: Grrrrrr!

Farmer Barnwell: Could I buy your fish?

Grizzly: Grrrrrr! *(Shakes head.)* Fish not for sale! *(Exits, growling and dragging his big fish.)*

Farmer Barnwell: Drat! What a day. No fish. Come on, Roly Worm. We're going home. Grandma Barnwell said there would be days like this. *(Pulls up his line with Roly Worm on it.)*

Roly Worm: Yes, I remember. There's always tomorrow to go fishing. Say, Farmer Barnwell, how about using a plastic worm tomorrow? Might change your luck. It sure would change mine!

Curtain.

Making a fish for *Gone Fishing.*

Props: four fishing poles, three fish, and Roly Worm (see instructions for all, pages 74–76)

See instructions for Grizzly puppet, pages 77–82.

Production notes: Slip fishing poles into Barnwell puppets' right sleeves. Tape pole to Grizzly's right paw.

How to Make Fish and Roly Worm

Make four fishing poles by tying a length of string to each dowel.

Photocopy the fish pictures and Roly Worm on pages 74 through 76. Color them and cut them out. Lay each cut-out picture on sturdy cardboard and trace around it. Cut shape out of cardboard and glue paper picture to the cardboard shape. Make a small hole in the mouth of each fish and one in the top of Roly Worm's head.

Each fish should be tied to the string of one fishing pole. Slip the string through the hole, then tie a knot in the string. Tie Roly Worm to the remaining pole.

Smallest fish caught by Martha Barnwell

Roly Worm

Middle size fish caught by Grandma Barnwell

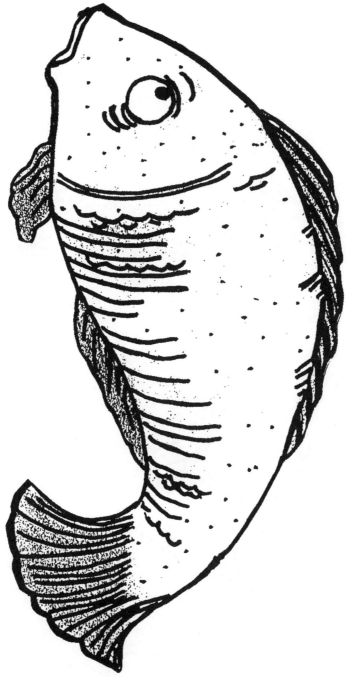

Big fish caught by Grizzly

How to Make a Grizzly Bear

Begin with a rectangular foam block and a 3" foam ball. Glue the ball to the block (it will be easier if you slice a bit off of the ball to give you a flat surface for gluing). Push a 12" wooden dowel into the bottom of the foam block.

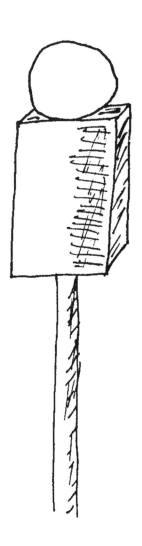

Grizzly bear — cone for nose
Cut 1 from brown felt, 1 from
cardboard

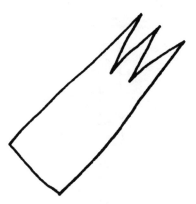

Grizzly bear claw — cut 2
from yellow felt

Grizzly bear arm — cut 2 from brown fur

Grizzly head — cut 1 of brown fur

Cut a 6" × 15" rectangle of brown furry fabric. Photocopy the patterns for the Grizzly on pages 78–79. Cut them out and use them to cut brown furry fabric for the arms and head; brown felt and cardboard (one of each) for the nose; and yellow felt for the claws. Drape the brown fur head piece over the foam ball and glue in place. Cut a red felt mouth and glue in place. Cut some white fangs and glue them to the front of the mouth. Form the cardboard nose piece into a cone by gluing the ends together. Glue brown felt over the cardboard cone. Poke the eyes in place and glue; do the same with the nose piece. Glue a plastic animal nose to tip of cone. Wrap the larger piece of brown fur around the styrofoam rectangle and glue in place. Fold each arm piece in half and glue in place at the top of the body just below the head. Glue claws at the ends of his arms.

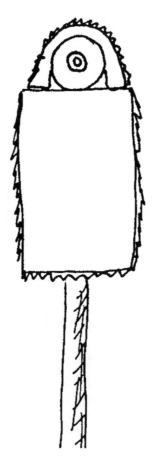

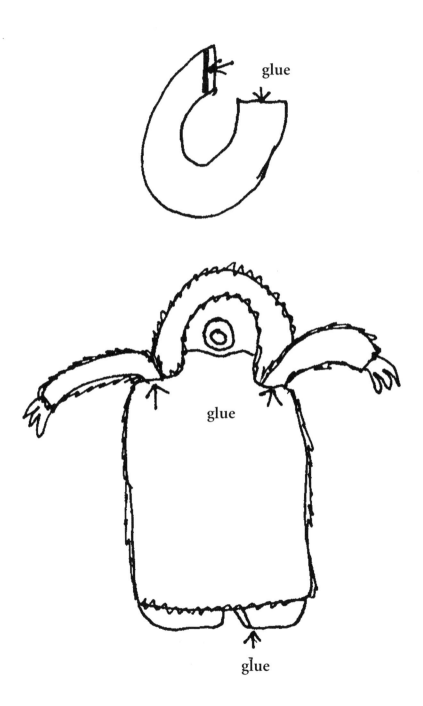

glue

glue

glue

Finished Grizzly dowel puppet

Talkabout

1. Have you ever gone fishing?
2. Where? Were you in a boat, on the land or walking in the water?
3. Did a big fish ever get away from you?
4. Did Farmer Barnwell catch any fish in the story?
   (No.)
5. Who did?
   (Martha Barnwell, Grandma Barnwell, and Grizzly.)
6. Have you ever seen a grizzly bear?
   (Tell children some facts about the grizzly: The grizzly bear is considered one of the most dangerous of bears. They have very bad tempers and sharp claws and teeth. The grizzly is bigger than the black bear. The Kodiak bear is larger than the grizzly.)
7. What color is the polar bear?
   (White.)
8. What are baby bears called?
   (Cubs.)
9. Have you seen a bear in a zoo or National Park?
10. Can bears climb trees?
    (Yes.)
11. Do bears go fishing?
    (Yes. They scoop the fish up with their paws.)
12. Did Grizzly let Farmer Barnwell buy his fish?
    (No.)
13. What did Grandma Barnwell tell Farmer Barnwell to make him feel better about not catching any fish?
    (She said, "Remember there is always tomorrow. There will be days like this. Don't give up.")
14. Were Martha Barnwell and Grandma happy about their fish?
    (Yes.)
15. Who else was happy?
    (Roly Worm.)
16. Why?
    (The fish didn't get a chance to gobble him up off Farmer Barnwell's fishing line. Roly suggested that Farmer Barnwell, in the future, use plastic worms.)

Camping Out

WHERE: Farmer Barnwell's backyard.   WHEN: Summer.   PUP-
PETS: Seven. Many lines in this play are spoken from offstage with no
puppets visible. The "Ghost" and "Bear" are Rosie and Daisy in disguise and should have the same voices as Rosie and Daisy.   TIME:
Approximately 10 minutes.

CHARACTERS

ROSIE BARNWELL. . . . Farmer Barnwell's daughter
                                            (twin to Daisy)
DAISY BARNWELL. . . . Farmer Barnwell's daughter
                                            (twin to Rosie)
BUD BARNWELL . . . . Older Barnwell brother
BOBBY BARNWELL . . . Younger Barnwell brother
GHOST . . . . Rosie Barnwell in disguise
BEAR. . . . . Daisy Barnwell in disguise
SKUNK

At Rise: Night. A black sky backdrop is decorated with stars and a half-
moon. A tent stands to one side of stage.

BUD: *(Enters from side opposite the tent.)* Get a move on, Bobby.
The girls will be here before you know it. If we pretend we're asleep,
they can't make us get out of the tent tonight.

BOBBY: *(Breathlessly enters.)* I'm coming as fast as I can. *(He car-
ries a large cake [see production notes].)* I don't want to drop this jelly
bean cake. It's awesome!

Ghost, Bear, and Skunk puppets on the set of *Camping Out*.

BUD: Does Mom know you have the cake?

BOBBY: No.

BUD: Thought so. Oh, well, let's jump into our sleeping bags, eat cake, and pretend we are asleep.

BOBBY: O.K., Bud. *(Boys go behind tent. [Remove cake from BOBBY's hands.] Lines are spoken behind tent.)*

BUD: Hurry up. Undo your sleeping bag.

BOBBY: I'm hurrying.

BUD: Oh! Oh! Watch out for the cake, you big ox. You almost sat on it.

BOBBY: I did not! And who are you calling a big ox?

BUD: Who do you think?

(ROSIE and DAISY enter and cross to tent.)

ROSIE: *(Shouts.)* Both you big oxes, scram out of that tent! It is our turn to camp out tonight, and you know it!

DAISY: You camped out last night. Right, Daisy?

ROSIE: Right, Sis.

BUD: *(Behind tent.)* Sorry, but we're settled in for the night and we're not moving. You girls can camp out tomorrow night.

ROSIE: But we want to camp out tonight!

DAISY: Those boys make me so mad. *(Looks up.)* Oh, look, Rosie. There's a new moon. Let's make a wish on it.

ROSIE: I wish those meanie, selfish boys would get kicked out of the tent tonight!

DAISY: That's my wish, too.

BUD: *(Behind tent.)* Not a chance. Goodnight, Bobby.

BOBBY: *(Behind tent.)* Goodnight, Bud. *(They snore.)*

ROSIE: It's not fair.

DAISY: Shall we tell Mom and Dad?

ROSIE: No. They're tired. Dad worked hard in the vegetable garden today, and Mom spent the day baking.

DAISY: Did you see the terrific cake she made? Best ever!

ROSIE: Let's go and have a piece.

DAISY: Good idea. *(They exit.)*

BUD: *(Sticks his head out of the tent.)* Those silly girls. They think they're going for Mom's cake, and we have it! Ha! Ha! on them. They think they are so smart because they're older than we are.

BOBBY: *(Sticks his head out of the tent.)* The girls will be mad that we have the cake.

BUD: Tough!

DAISY: *(Enters.)* Those dirty rats! Those boys stole the cake! They took the cake *and* took our turn for the tent!

ROSIE: *(Enters.)* They have been stuffing their fat faces with Mom's great cake, and we haven't had a bite.

BUD: *(Whispers.)* Quick! Get back in the tent! Here come the girls. *(They go behind the tent and start snoring.)*

DAISY: *(Whispers.)* Can you think of something we can do to get them out of the tent?

ROSIE: I've got an idea.

DAISY: What?

ROSIE: *(Whispers.)* We will scare them out.

DAISY: *(Loudly.)* How?

ROSIE: *(Whispers.)* Sh! Follow me. *(The girls exit.)*

BUD: *(Sticks his head out of the tent.)* They're gone.

BOBBY: *(Sticks his head out of the tent.)* Do you think they have given up and gone to bed in the house?

BUD: Yep. We can go to sleep now. It's a great night for camping out. *(They go back behind the tent.)*

BOBBY: *(Moans from behind the tent.)* Oh! Oh! Oh! My stomach hurts!

BUD: Don't be a baby. You ate too much jelly bean cake. Go to sleep!

GHOST: *(Enters.)* OOOOOOOOOO! *(Flies around stage.)*

BOBBY: *(From behind the tent.)* What was that?

BUD: Probably an old screech owl. Go to sleep!

ROSIE: *(Enters and whispers to* GHOST.*)* You make a great ghost, Daisy!

GHOST/DAISY: *(Whispers.)* Thanks, Rosie. *(Flies around.)* OOO-OOOOOOOOOOOOOOOOOOOO!

*(*ROSIE *hides in one corner of stage.)*

BOBBY: *(Sticks his head out of the tent.)* Yikes! That's no owl! Bud, come look! It's a g-g-g-ghost!

BUD: *(Sticks his head out of the tent.)* Cut the kidding.

BOBBY: I'm not kidding. See? There's a real, live ghost floating around out there!

BUD: There's no such thing as ghosts.

BOBBY: Then what do you call that w-w-w-white thing floating around?

BUD: Hey, wait a minute. That's no ghost. That's one of the twins. I can tell by the way she's jumping around. The girls are trying to scare us out of the tent.

BOBBY: She sure scared me. *(Goes behind the tent.)*

BUD: Didn't scare me. You're just a scaredy cat. *(Goes behind the tent.)*

ROSIE: *(Whispers.)* The ghost trick didn't work.

GHOST/DAISY: What do we do now?

ROSIE: I have another plan. *(They exit.)*

BUD: *(Sticks his head out of the tent.)* The twins must feel silly that their ghost trick was a flop.

BOBBY: *(Sticks his head out of the tent.)* Silly is right.

BUD: Let's have another piece of jelly bean cake.

BOBBY: Now you're talking! *(They go behind the tent.)*

*(*BEAR *enters.)*

DAISY: *(Enters and speaks to* BEAR*)*. You make a super bear, Rosie.

BEAR/ROSIE: I hope the bear trick works to scare those guys out of the tent better than the ghost trick did.

DAISY: You will scare them out of their wits in that bear outfit.

BEAR/ROSIE: Hope so.

DAISY: Growl loud, like a fierce bear, Rosie.

BEAR/ROSIE: How's this? GRRRRRRRRRRRRR!

DAISY: Great! Do it again, only louder and fiercer.

BEAR/ROSIE: GRRRRRRRRRRRRRRR!

BUD: *(From behind the tent.)* What was that?

BOBBY: *(From behind the tent.)* I-I-I-I didn't hear anything.

BUD: You did, too. Listen.

BEAR/ROSIE: GRRRRRRRRR!

BUD: That GRRRRRR sounds like … a bear.

BOBBY: A bear! A real, live bear outside our tent?

BUD: Let's get out of here!

BEAR/ROSIE: GRRRRRRRRRRR!

(DAISY hides in one corner of stage.)

BUD: *(Sticks his head out of the tent.)* B-B-B-Bobby! T-T-There *is* a big b-b-b-bear outside the tent!

BOBBY: *(Sticks his head out of the tent.)* Yikers! *(Very excited.)* It *is* a bear!

BUD: Now, don't get excited. Keep calm. Keep your cool. I know what we will do.

BOBBY: What?

BUD: We'll sweet talk the beast.

BOBBY: How do you do that?

BUD: Watch me. *(Politely.)* Hello, Mr. Bear.

BEAR/ROSIE: GRRRRRRRRR!

BUD: Nice bear. Handsome bear. You don't want to claw us to pieces, do you? Not two nice guys like us.

(BEAR/ROSIE growls very loud and starts toward the tent.)

BOBBY: *(Whispers.)* Your sweet talk isn't working.

BUD: Then we'll have to make a dash for the house, faster than the bear can catch us.

BOBBY: M-M-M-My legs won't move.

BUD: You'd better move when I say go, or else. Ready? Go! *(The boys run out of the tent and exit.)*

(BEAR/ROSIE *laughs.*)

DAISY: *(Enters.)* We sure fooled those two this time. You made a great bear, Rosie.

BEAR/ROSIE: Thanks, Daisy. Let's go in the tent and have some cake and get some shut-eye. I'm tired after all the excitement.

DAISY: I'm with you. *(They go behind the tent and speak their lines from there.)* Hmmmm! Mom's cake *is* the best.

ROSIE: Sure is. Glad to get this bear suit off.

DAISY: This is a perfect night for camping out. Our wish on the new moon came true.

ROSIE: It sure did. Goodnight, Daisy.

DAISY: Goodnight, Rosie. I guess we proved girls are smarter than boys any day.

ROSIE: You never said a truer word.

(SKUNK *enters. Walks across the stage, sniffing at things. Goes to the tent. Goes inside the tent.*)

ROSIE and DAISY: *(Screaming loudly from behind tent.)* A skunk!

ROSIE: There's a skunk in our tent!

DAISY: What will we do?

ROSIE: Sweet talk it.

DAISY: How do you do that?

ROSIE: Like this. *(Politely.)* Hello, Mr. Skunk. You're a handsome skunk. You have beautiful white and black fur. Want a piece of cake?

DAISY: Cut the sweet talk. We'd better get out. You know what skunks do?

ROSIE: Right! *(Dashes out of tent and exits.* DAISY *also dashes out of tent and exits.)*

SKUNK: *(Comes out of tent and walks around.)* Looks like *I* get the tent tonight! What a beautiful night for camping out!

Curtain.

———————————————

Props: Jelly bean cake (see instructions, pages 91–92), tent (see instructions, page 90)

See instructions for Ghost, Bear, and Skunk puppets on pages 92–95.

Production notes: Cake is taped to Bobby's hands at beginning of play. Remove it when he goes behind tent for the first time.

How to Make the Tent

On green construction paper, using the drawing below as a model, draw a tent shape that measures 10" from the tallest point to the bottom. (You can make it larger or smaller to suit your stage.) Cut it out and trace it onto a piece of cardboard. Glue the construction paper tent to this cardboard backing for support.

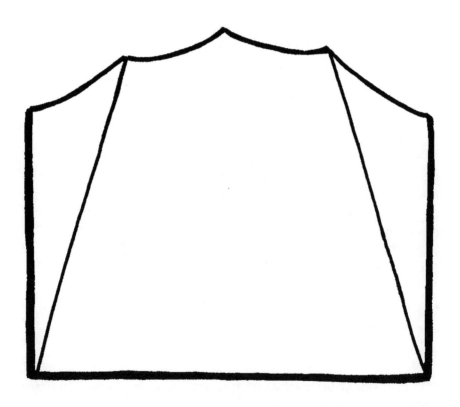

How to Make the Jelly Bean Cake

1. Cut a circle 3 inches in diameter out of thin cardboard. Cut a strip of paper or felt, 2" wide by 9" long. Cut a round piece of felt or paper, for the top of the cake 3" in diameter.

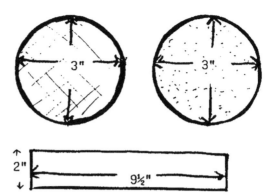

2. Glue the long strip around the edges of the cardboard circle.

3. Glue the round piece of felt to the top of the cake. leave an opening. Stuff with cotton balls.

4. Glue the opening closed. Cut jelly bean shapes out of different colored paper or felt, and glue to the top of the cake.

How to Make a Ghost

Take a small foam ball and poke a hole in one end. Insert a dowel rod into hole, gluing in place. Cut a 12" × 10" rectangle of white cheesecloth. Drape over ball and dowel, tying a string below ball to keep cloth in place and give ghost a neck. Draw or glue on eyes.

How to Make a Bear

See instructions for making Grizzly puppet on pages 77–82.

How to Make a Skunk

Begin with an empty toilet paper tube. Make a small hole in the center of one side and insert a 12" wooden dowel in the hole. Attach a thin strip of cardboard to one end (this will be the tail).

Photocopy the pattern and use it to cut a body out of black felt. Cover the toilet paper tube with the felt, gluing felt in place. Stretch and glue felt over one end to make a round face. Glue on roly eyes, or use buttons for eyes. Cut a round nose from pink felt and glue in place. Now cut a long strip of white felt or furry fabric, long enough to extend along the back and over the cardboard strip. Glue in place.

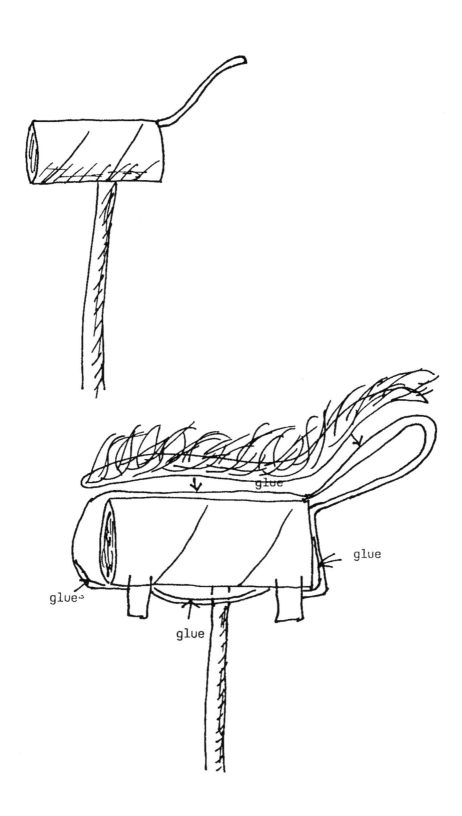

glue

glue

glue

glue

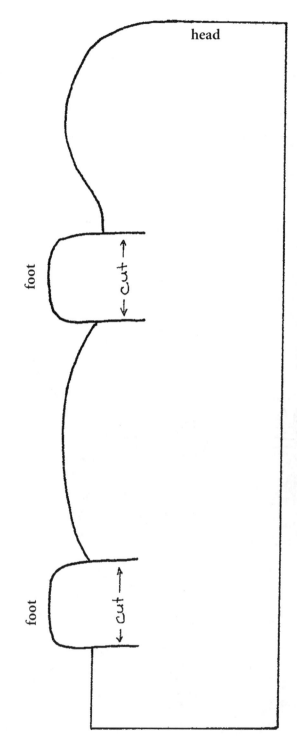

Skunk body — cut 1 on fold of black felt

head

foot

foot

Cut

Cut

place this edge on fold — do not cut

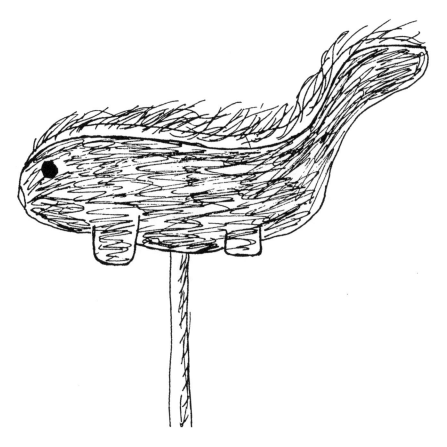

Finished Skunk dowel puppet

Talkabout

1. How many of you have slept outdoors in a tent?
2. Did you like camping out?
3. Did you ever feel that something strange was outside your tent?
4. In the play, why were Rosie and Daisy mad at the boys?
   (The boys had camped out the night before, and it was the girls'
   turn. The girls were even madder when they found out the boys
   had the jelly bean cake!)
5. What did the girls do to try to frighten their brothers out of the tent?
   (They pretended to be a ghost and a bear.)

6. Who won in the end?
     (Skunk!)
7. Have you ever wished on the new moon?
8. Did you know the moon is about 238,855 miles from the earth?
   The moon is about one-fourth the size of the earth. Does the moon
   travel around the earth?
     (Yes, at an average speed of 2,300 mph.)
9. Are there mountains and craters on the moon?
     (Yes.)
10. How long is a day on the moon?
     (About two weeks. More moon facts: We see only one side of
     the moon; the moon is the earth's nearest neighbor. The moon
     travels all the way around the earth in a little less than a month.)
11. What is an eclipse of the moon?
     (It happens when the moon passes through the earth's shadow.
     The earth is between the moon and the sun.)
12. When the girls wished on the new moon, did their wish come true?
   Could you wish on a full moon or a half moon as well?

Who Stole the Pie?

WHERE: Farmer Barnwell's barn.   WHEN: Summer.   PUPPETS:
Five.   TIME: Approximately 10 minutes.

CHARACTERS

FARMER BARNWELL. . . Owner of the Barnwell Farm
MARTHA BARNWELL . . Farmer Barnwell's wife
WATCHDOG . . . . . . Barnwells' dog
BIG DETECTIVE
   SLEUTH SLICKER. . . Big City detective
RACKY RACCOON
SKUNKY

At Rise: A natural burlap backdrop represents the inside of Farmer Barnwell's barn. Martha Barnwell is standing by a big blueberry pie center
stage. She has just put it on the shelf in the barn. Watchdog stands off
to one side of stage.

———————————

MARTHA BARNWELL: I am hiding my blueberry pie here in the barn
so nobody will eat it before tonight. Harry likes blueberry pie better than
cake for his birthday. *(Goes to Watchdog.)* Now listen up, Watchdog, I
want you to guard this pie.
WATCHDOG: Arf! Arf!
MARTHA BARNWELL: Do you understand? Guard this blueberry pie
with your life. No one gets this pie except my husband, Harry.
WATCHDOG: Arf! Arf!

The cast of *Who Stole the Pie?*

MARTHA BARNWELL: Good dog, Watchdog. I know I can depend on you. *(Exits.)*

WATCHDOG: Think I'll take a little nap. No one will take the pie. They don't even know it's here. *(Drops off stage.)*

(The pie slides off the stage [pulled by a string].)

WATCHDOG: *(Pops up.)* Arf! Arf! It's great what a little shut-eye will do for you. *(He goes to where the pie had been. He barks wildly.)* Woof! Woof! The pie! The pie is gone! I was only napping a minute. Mrs. Barnwell will have my hide. Wait until she finds out!

MARTHA BARNWELL: *(Enters.)* What will I find out?

WATCHDOG: That your blueberry pie is gone! Vanished!

MARTHA BARNWELL: Impossible! You were guarding it! You didn't take your eye off that pie for a second—did you?

WATCHDOG: W-w-well …

MARTHA BARNWELL: Well, did you?

WATCHDOG: Maybe for one *tiny* second.

MARTHA BARNWELL: How could you? You knew how important it was to guard that pie today.

WATCHDOG: It was only one short nap. When I woke up, the pie was gone. Somebody must have stolen the pie while I was asleep.

MARTHA BARNWELL: I am so upset, I could scream!

WATCHDOG: Please don't.

MARTHA BARNWELL: Yes, I will! *(She screams loudly.)*

BIG DETECTIVE SLEUTH SLICKER: *(Enters.)* Did someone scream?

MARTHA BARNWELL: I did. Who are you?

SLEUTH SLICKER: I am Big Detective Sleuth Slicker at your service. What is your problem?

MARTHA BARNWELL: Someone stole the blueberry pie I made for my husband's birthday today.

SLEUTH SLICKER: Where did you have the pie?

MARTHA BARNWELL: I hid it here in the barn, so no one would find it. I even had our dog, Watchdog, guard it.

SLEUTH SLICKER: Some watchdog. How is it a thief stole the pie from under his watchful eye?

MARTHA BARNWELL: He took a short nap.

SLEUTH SLICKER: Oh, I see.

MARTHA BARNWELL: I think I'm going to cry.

SLEUTH SLICKER: Please don't do that. Crying women make me nervous. Never mind, I'll find your pie. I'm a great detective. Everybody knows that.

WATCHDOG: I don't.

SLEUTH SLICKER: Let's get down to business and solve this mystery. *(Goes to Watchdog.)* Watchdog, did you steal Mrs. Barnwell's blueberry pie?

WATCHDOG: I did not!

SLEUTH SLICKER: You look most suspicious. You have a blue tongue.

WATCHDOG: My tongue is always blue.

SLEUTH SLICKER: A likely tale.

(RACKY RACCOON enters.)

SLEUTH SLICKER: Upon my detective badge, there's your thief. I know a thief when I see one. He is wearing a black mask.

MARTHA BARNWELL: That is Racky Raccoon. All raccoons wear a black mask.

SLEUTH SLICKER: A likely tale. *(Goes to Racky Raccoon.)* Tell me now, Racky Raccoon, did you steal the blueberry pie?

RACKY RACCOON: No, I didn't.

SLEUTH SLICKER: How come there are blue steaks on your white fur? Looks like blueberry juice to me.

RACKY RACCOON: I've always had blue streaks on my white fur.

SLEUTH SLICKER: A likely tale. *(Goes to Mrs. Barnwell.)* Did *you* steal the blueberry pie, Mrs. Barnwell?

MARTHA BARNWELL: Upon my soul and body! Why would I steal my own pie?

SLEUTH SLICKER: You might have been hungry for a piece of blueberry pie.

MARTHA BARNWELL: Definitely not! The pie is for my husband's birthday.

SLEUTH SLICKER: All right. If Watchdog didn't steal the pie, and if Racky Raccoon didn't steal the pie, and if you didn't steal the pie, Mrs. Barnwell, then who did?

MARTHA BARNWELL: Maybe, just by chance, Mr. Big Detective did.

SLEUTH SLICKER: Me? The big captain of the Big City Detective Force? Me, my good woman, steal a measly blueberry pie?

MARTHA BARNWELL: Did you?

SLEUTH SLICKER: I most certainly did not! I feel insulted.

MARTHA BARNWELL: There are blue stains on the white handkerchief in your coat pocket.

SLEUTH SLICKER: They have been there a long time!

WATCHDOG: A likely tale.

MARTHA BARNWELL: I know what we'll do. We'll let the audience decide the case. *(Turns to audience.)* Audience, did Watchdog steal the blueberry pie?

(Audience answers.)

MARTHA BARNWELL: *(Goes to Racky Raccoon.)* Did Racky Raccoon steal the pie?

(Audience answers.)

SLEUTH SLICKER: *(Goes to Martha Barnwell.)* Did Martha Barnwell steal her own pie?

(Audience answers.)

MARTHA BARNWELL: Did Big Detective Sleuth Slicker steal my blueberry pie?

(Audience answers.)

SLEUTH SLICKER: Who stole the pie? Call out the guilty party.

(Audience calls out names. There is a big commotion.)

FARMER BARNWELL: *(Enters.)* What in the wide world is going on in my barn? I could hear you way down in South Pasture. Please, everyone be quiet. Sh! Sh!

SLEUTH SLICKER: You must be Farmer Barnwell.

FARMER BARNWELL: I am. And who might you be?

SLEUTH SLICKER: I am Big Detective Sleuth Slicker on vacation from Big City. I was passing by and heard someone scream. I came in to help.

MARTHA BARNWELL: Someone stole the blueberry pie I made for your birthday.

FARMER BARNWELL: Is that what all this fuss is about? No one stole the blueberry pie.

MARTHA BARNWELL: Then where is it? It's gone from here in the barn where I left it.

FARMER BARNWELL: Oh, I'm sorry I'm the cause of this commotion. I knew it was for me, so I took it down to the South Pasture to eat it while I worked. I couldn't wait until tonight for a piece. Say, how would you all like a piece of my birthday pie right now?

SLEUTH SLICKER: I detect a great idea!

WATCHDOG: Arf! Arf!

MARTHA BARNWELL: I would want a piece. I do make delicious blueberry pie.

RACKY RACCOON: *(Jumps up and down.)* Me too! Me too!

FARMER BARNWELL: O.K. Follow me to South Pasture and have a super treat. *(All exit.)*

[The pie is pushed up center stage and SKUNKY's *head appears.)*

SKUNKY: That super treat is no longer in South Pasture. It's going down into my mouth piece by piece, because it's *my* birthday too! I know this is the best blueberry pie I ever had for my birthday. *(He sniffs the pie then sings.)* Happy birthday to me! Happy birthday to me! Happy birthday, dear Skunky. Happy birthday to me!

Curtain.

Props: Blueberry pie (see instructions on pages 102–103).

See instructions for Watchdog, Racky Raccoon, and Sleuth Slicker puppets on pages 104–115. See instructions for Skunky on pages 92–95.

How to Make a Blueberry Pie

1. From thin cardboard, cut a circle 3" in diameter. Cut a strip 1½" wide by 11" long. Glue the strip around the circle, forming the pie plate.

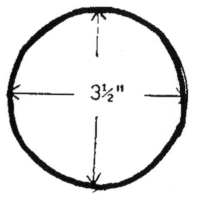

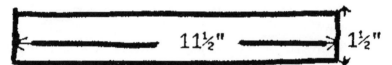

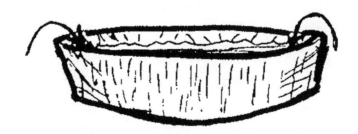

2. Cover the pie plate with aluminum foil, bringing it to the inside of the plate. Secure with glue if necessary.

3. Cut a circle of light blue felt slightly larger than the pie plate. Place in pie plate and secure to top edge with glue, leaving one side open. Stuff pie with cotton balls. Finish gluing all the way.

4. Dip the end of a pencil into dark blue paint and dab it onto the top of the pie so it looks like blueberries.

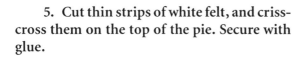

5. Cut thin strips of white felt, and crisscross them on the top of the pie. Secure with glue.

How to Make
Detective Sleuth Slicker

Begin with a ½" wood dowel, about 12" long. Push dowel into a round or egg-shaped foam ball (about 2½" is a good size for the ball, which will be your puppet's head). You may wish to glue the ball onto the dowel to keep it secure.

Now make Sleuth Slicker's face by attaching eyes (they can be roly eyes from a craft store, or felt), nose (a red bead), and mouth (red felt). Add hair and mustache (wig hair, yarn, or some other artificial hair).

Add a small hat (if you can't find a yellow one, buy a natural straw hat and paint it yellow). Glue to head. Add a black ribbon hatband; glue in place. Now you can begin to dress the dowel.

Photocopy or trace the raincoat and hand pattern on page 105 and Farmer Barnwell's pants pattern on page 21. Cut all patterns out and lay them on fabric, using black felt for the pants and yellow felt for the raincoat; use your choice of felt for the hands.

All the clothing pieces are glued together inside out and then turned right side out when the glue dries. Begin with the pants: Glue the outer seams first, then the middle seam, leaving an opening in the middle for the dowel to come through. Turn right side out and set aside.

To make the raincoat, after cutting out the two pieces, cut one of

Sleuth Slicker's raincoat —
cut 2 on fold

place this line on fold, do not cut

Hand — cut 2

the pieces in half, cutting up the center; this will be the front of the rain-coat. Glue the front pieces to the back along the sides and under the arms; then glue the shoulder seams across the top, leaving an opening for the neck. Turn right side out. Glue the hands into the ends of the sleeves.

Push an empty toilet paper tube into the pants and glue the pants to the tube. Put the bottom of the dowel into the toilet paper tube, pushing it through the opening left in the pants. Wrap the raincoat around the tube, then push a little stuffing into the sleeves and shoulders. Turn down the top corners of the raincoat front to look like lapels; glue in place. Cut a white piece of felt or other cloth to fit into the neck of the raincoat, covering the stuffing; it should look like a shirt. Glue in place.

To make the necktie, cut a strip of black felt about 6" long. Wrap around neck once and glue in place; then tie ends into a bow and glue bow in place on front of neck.

Finish by placing a strip of yellow felt around his middle for a belt. Cut out a belt buckle shape from black felt and glue to the belt. Put glue on the belt buckle and sprinkle gold glitter to it. Glue a small piece of white felt to the raincoat front for a handkerchief. Add a couple of blue lines on a white hankerchief.

Finished Sleuth Slicker dowel puppet

How to Make the Watchdog

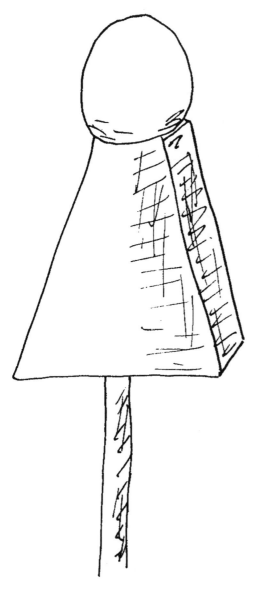

1. Begin with a block of foam. Using a knife or scissors, shape it into a square-based pyramid and lop off the point to make it flat on top. Insert a dowel into the base of this shape, and glue a foam ball to the top (slice a bit off the ball to give you a flat base to work with).

2. Using patterns on following page, cut front paws and ears from brown, furry fabric; cut mouth from red felt; cut tongue from blue felt.

3. With a piece of tan felt, cover the body you have made from the foam pieces. Glue on ears, front legs, mouth, and tongue. Add roly eyes or eyes cut from felt. Add a small plastic nose or a nose cut from felt.

4. If you have an old watch you can spare, place it around your Watchdog's neck with the clock face forward. If not, cut a watch face from a magazine and glue it under his chin; add a silver ribbon for a band.

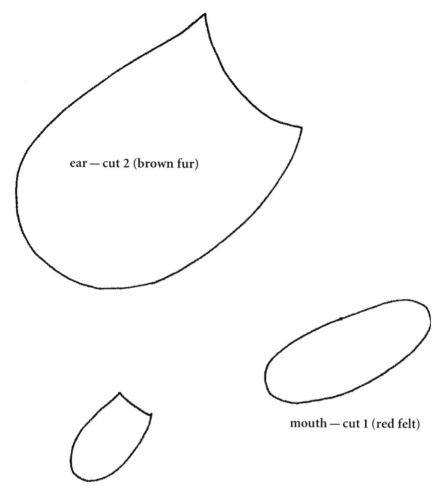

ear — cut 2 (brown fur)

mouth — cut 1 (red felt)

tonguc — cut 1 (blue felt)

front legs — cut 2 (brown fur)

The Watchdog

How to Make Racky Raccoon

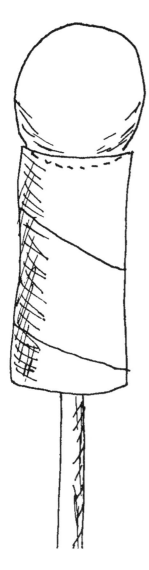

1. Begin with a 3" foam ball. Insert a dowel into ball (glue in place if needed), then drop dowel through an empty toilet paper tube so that foam ball rests in top of tube and dowel protrudes from bottom of tube.

2. Using patterns on the following pages, cut raccoon body and ears from tan, furry fabric; cut face and belly from white, furry fabric; cut mask from black felt.

3. Wrap body piece around the body you have made from the toilet paper tube and foam ball, leaving room to stuff body with cotton or other stuffing. Glue body fabric to paper towel roll. Stuff raccoon to plump him up. Glue on face, belly, ears, and mask. Add roly eyes or felt eyes, a plastic or felt nose, and a red felt mouth. Add blue streaks to his belly with ink or fabric paint.

4. For the tail, cut 3 black and 3 tan fur strips 6" long by 2" wide. Curl each into a tube and glue edge. Now glue the tubes together, alternating colors, starting with tan and ending in black. Glue tail to body, starting in the back and bringing tail around to the front.

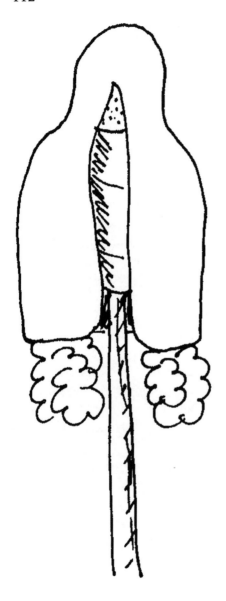

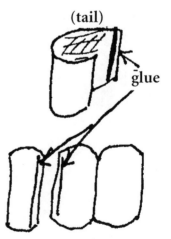

(tail)

glue

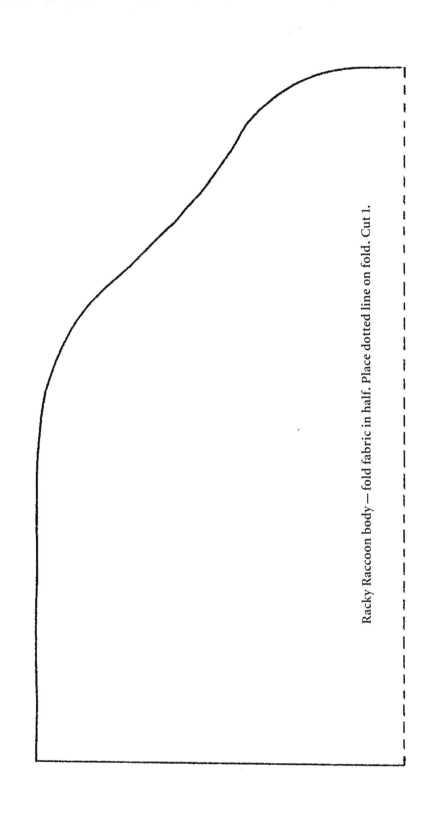

Racky Raccoon body — fold fabric in half. Place dotted line on fold. Cut 1.

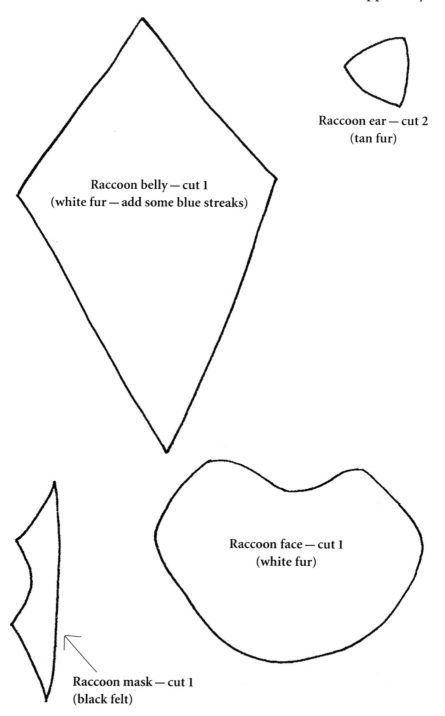

Raccoon ear — cut 2
(tan fur)

Raccoon belly — cut 1
(white fur — add some blue streaks)

Raccoon face — cut 1
(white fur)

Raccoon mask — cut 1
(black felt)

Finished Racky Raccoon dowel puppet

Talkabout

1. Why did Martha Barnwell make a blueberry pie?
   (It was her husband's birthday, and Farmer Barnwell loved blueberry pie better than cake.)
2. Why did Martha Barnwell hide the newly baked pie in the barn?

(She didn't want anyone to eat it before the birthday dinner that night. Besides, it was a surprise.)
3. Who did Martha Barnwell get to guard the pie?
    (Watchdog.)
4. Did Watchdog do a good job?
    (No.)
5. What happened?
    (Watchdog took a little nap and someone stole the pie.)
6. Who came along to help find the guilty party?
    (Big Detective Sleuth Slicker, who was on vacation from Big City.)
7. Who were the suspects?
    (Watchdog, Racky Raccoon, Martha Barnwell, and Sleuth Slicker himself.)
8. Did any of you guess who stole the pie?
9. Should you say someone is guilty of stealing something before he is proven guilty of stealing?
    (No.)
10. What were the clues to make each suspect seem guilty?
    (Watchdog had a blue tongue. Racky Raccoon had blue streaks on his fur. Sleuth Slicker had blue on his white handkerchief. Martha Barnwell could be guilty because she knew where the pie was.)
11. Who took the pie?
    (Farmer Barnwell took the pie.)
12. Why?
    (He knew the blueberry pie was for his birthday, and he couldn't wait.)
13. Do you call this stealing?
14. Do you like cake or pie better?
15. What is your favorite pie?
16. Stealing something is not worth the stealing. Why?
    (It makes you feel bad even if you say it doesn't. You always have to worry about someone finding out you stole. You could be punished or even go to jail.)
17. Who ended up with the blueberry pie?
    (Skunky)
18. Is Skunky a thief?
    (Discussion)

Froggie Woggies

WHERE: Frog Pond.   WHEN: Spring.   PUPPETS: Ten. (One character, Bully Frog, is represented by two different puppets — the normal Bully Frog and the "Mosquito-Bitten" Bully Frog. These puppets should be operated by the same puppeteer.)   TIME: Approximately 10 minutes.

CHARACTERS

FARMER BARNWELL. . . Owner of the Barnwell Farm
BOGGY WOG. . . . . . A good-guy frog
BULLY FROG . . . . . . A frog who sometimes gets into trouble
LILY FROG . . . . Girlfriend of Boggy Wog
FROGETTE . . . . A dancer at the Spider Web Cafe
ZAPPER. . . . . Another dancer at the Spider Web Cafe
FLAME . . . . A singer at the Spider Web Cafe
CRUSHER. . . . . A mean old snapping turtle
MONSTER MOSQUITO . A giant mosquito
MOSQUITO-BITTEN
   BULLY FROG. . . . . Swollen to giant size from mosquito bites

At Rise: A blue sky backdrop is dotted with white clouds. Frog sounds (chirps, ribbits, and gurrumps) are coming from all sides of the stage. Lily pads are scattered here and there. Boggy Wog is center stage talking with his girlfriend, Lily Frog.

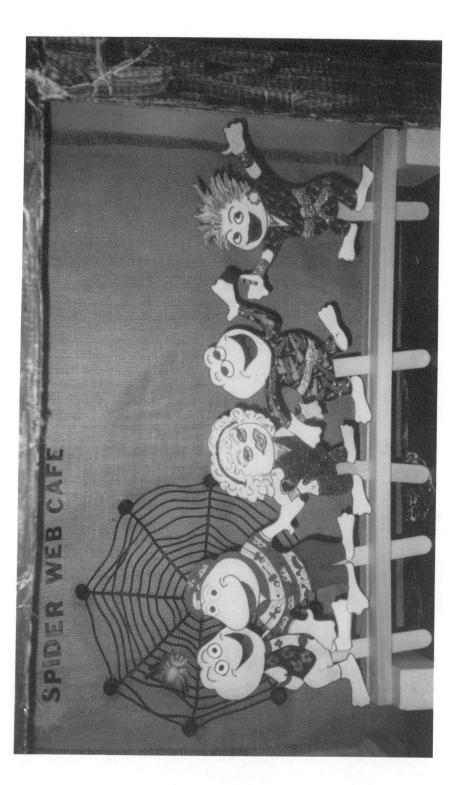

BOGGY WOG: Gurrrump.

LILY FROG: *(Stands close to Boggy Wog and speaks with a sweet voice.)* Gurrrrrrump.

BOGGY WOG: You have neat froggie eyes, Lily Frog. Ribbit.

LILY FROG: *(Sweetly.)* Thank you, Boggy Wog. You have neat froggie eyes, too. Ribbit. Ribbit.

BOGGY WOG: You are a high froggie jumper.

LILY FROG: You are the highest froggie jumper in Frog Pond, Boggy Wog.

BOGGY WOG: I can jump higher than Bully Frog.

LILY FROG: I know you can.

BULLY FROG: *(Jumps in.)* You can what?

BOGGY WOG: Oh, nothing, Bully Frog.

LILY FROG: Boggy Wog says he can jump higher than you.

BULLY FROG: *(Jumps very close to Boggy Wog.)* Oh, yeah?

BOGGY WOG: *(Jumps back.)* Just fooling, Bully Frog. Everyone knows *you* are the best jumper in Frog Pond.

BULLY FROG: That's more like it. *(Jumps to Lily Frog. Talks sweetly.)* Hello, Lily Frog. For the life of me I don't see what you see in that Boggy Wog when I'm around. *(Speaks to Boggy Wog.)* Come on, Boggy Wog, we said we'd go mosquito catching. I'm hungry for a big mosquito.

LILY FROG: *(Jumps up and down.)* Let me go, too. I love to catch mosquitoes.

BULLY FROG: Naw! We want to go by ourselves.

LILY FROG: But I can jump as high as you can jump. *(Jumps high.)*

BULLY FROG: Forget it. Come on, Boggy Wog. Time to go.

BOGGY WOG: *(Sadly.)* Bye, Lily Frog. See you later. *(Exits jumping.)*

LILY FROG: Remember, don't go near Spider Web Cafe.

BULLY FROG: We will if we want. *(Jumps off stage.)*

FARMER BARNWELL: *(Enters.)* Top of the morning to you, Lily Frog. My! My! You are looking mighty pretty.

LILY FROG: *(Sadly.)* Thank you, Farmer Barnwell. *(She takes a few low jumps around the stage.)* Gurrump! Gurrump!

Opposite: From the play "Froggie Woggies." At the Spider Web Cafe with *(left to right)* Boggy Wog, Bully Frog, Frogette, Zapper, and Flame.

FARMER BARNWELL: Is there something bothering you?

LILY FROG: *(Jumping.)* Gurrump! Why do you ask?

FARMER BARNWELL: All I hear is gurrump, gurrump. You are not jumping high this morning, and it's a gorgeous day for high jumping. Wish I could high jump like a froggie woggie!

LILY FROG: I am froggie mad!

FARMER BARNWELL: Why are you froggie mad?

LILY FROG: Because I want to go mosquito catching with the boys.

FARMER BARNWELL: Never mind them, Lily Frog. Go out and do your own mosquito catching. There are some big mosquitoes at the south end of the pond.

LILY FROG: Thank you, Farmer Barnwell. Think I will go and catch a big mosquito and show those two wide-mouth frogs who's the best mosquito catcher. *(Jumps off stage.)*

FARMER BARNWELL: *(Calling to her.)* Any time, pretty frog. Any time. Oh, Lily Frog —?

LILY FROG: *(Jumps back on stage.)* Yes, Farmer Barnwell?

FARMER BARNWELL: Remember, do not go near the Spider Web Cafe. It is not the place for my froggie woggies.

LILY FROG: I will remember, Farmer Barnwell. *(Jumps off stage.)*

FARMER BARNWELL: *(Calling after her.)* Good girl, Lily! Good luck! *(Curtain closes.)*

SCENE 2

(Curtain opens. The backdrop now is green. A sign reading "Spider Web Cafe" hangs from backdrop. BOGGY WOG *and* BULLY FROG *are on-stage.)*

BOGGY WOG: We shouldn't be here, Bully Frog. You know we have been warned never to go near the Spider Web Cafe.

BULLY FROG: Oh, phooey. What does Farmer Barnwell know about it? Besides, it can't do any harm to look around the Spider Web Cafe. I hear the biggest mosquitoes hang out here.

BOGGY WOG: Think I'll go home, Bully Frog.

BULLY FROG: Sissy frog!

(Humming noise. MONSTER MOSQUITO *flies on stage.)*

BULLY FROG: *(Leans back.)* Wow! Look at that monster mosquito. What did I tell you? That's some big bug!

(MONSTER MOSQUITO *flies around the stage with a great humming noise.*)

BOGGY WOG: L-l-let's get out of here. That flying monster can bite big!

BULLY FROG: Not me. I'm not afraid of any big mosquito. I'm going to catch him before I go home. I want mosquito meat for dinner.

BOGGY WOG: He's probably tough eating.

BULLY FROG: Naw! The bigger, the better.

BOGGY WOG: He's too big. I'm going home.

(MONSTER MOSQUITO *flies off stage.*)

FLAME: *(Slides in with a mike in her hand.)* Oh, no, you're not, you cute froggie. Hello, handsome. I am Flame, the hottest singer around. What's your name?

BOGGY WOG: I'm Boggy Wog.

FROGETTE: *(Jumps on stage. She goes to Bully Frog.)* Hello, big frog, what's your name? My name is Frogette.

BULLY FROG: I'm Bully Frog.

(Loud music is heard backstage. ZAPPER *jumps up on stage and dances with* FROGETTE.*)*

FROGETTE: Get those frog legs moving, Bully Frog.

BULLY FROG: *(Starts to dance.)* Come on, dance, Boggy Wog. This is living!

BOGGY WOG: Think I'll go home.

BULLY FROG: Watch me high jump, Boggy Wog! *(Dances up a storm.)*

FLAME: *(Sings in a loud, raspy voice.)* The flame in my heart will burn, burn, burn. *(She jumps all over the stage.)* I will light a flame in your heart that will burn, burn, burn. Burn! Burn! Burn!

BOGGY WOG: Think I'll go home. I'm going back to Frog Pond.

BULLY FROG: Run on home, little froggy. I'm staying! Frog Pond is too dull for me. *(Music plays louder. Flame sings louder. Dancers dance harder.)*

(CRUSHER *enters and crawls in slowly. He crawls to Bully Frog.*)

BULLY FROG: Who's that? *(Still dancing.)*

ZAPPER: Who's who? *(Still dancing.)*

BULLY FROG: *(Still dancing.)* Who's that? *(Goes towards* CRUSHER.*)*

FLAME: *(Shrieks.)* It's Crusher, the snapping turtle! Jump for your lives! Crusher likes frog legs for dinner.

(FROGS *jump off stage very fast.*)

CRUSHER: I'll get 'em! I always do. Nothing like having frog legs for dinner tonight.

(Curtain closes.)

SCENE 3

(*Curtain opens on Froggie Wog Hollow as in Scene 1. Once again the sky is blue and the frogs are chirping, ribbitting and gurrumping from all sides of the stage. Lily pads are here and there.* BOGGY WOG *and* FARMER BARNWELL *are talking.*)

BOGGY WOG: I'm worried about my pal, Bully Frog.

FARMER BARNWELL: You should be. You say he is at the Spider Web Cafe? I have warned all young frogs over and over not to go to that place.

BOGGY WOG: Yes, but Bully Frog wouldn't come home with me. He likes it there. He thinks Frog Pond is a dull place.

FARMER BARNWELL: Silly frog. He has a lot to learn.

(Humming noise heard from backstage.)

BOGGY WOG: What is that humming?

FARMER BARNWELL: It sounds like a giant mosquito. Run for your life! (FARMER BARNWELL *and* BOGGY WOG *jump quickly below stage.*)

BULLY FROG: *(Floats on stage through the air, like a balloon.)* Hi, guys. It's me, Bully Frog.

(BOGGY WOG *and* FARMER BARNWELL *poke their heads up.*)

BOGGY WOG: *(Looks around.)* I don't see anyone.

FARMER BARNWELL: *(Leans back.)* I see a *huge* balloon. That's strange … that balloon looks familiar.

BOGGY WOG: Gollywoggles! It's Bully Frog, and he is blown up like a blimp. See the spots on him? He's coming in for a landing.

BULLY FROG: *(Lands on the stage.)* Phew! Glad to be home. Never did catch one of those miserable monster mosquitoes. But one of them bit me again and again! I've got mosquito bites all over me.

BOGGY WOG: You look awful!

BULLY FROG: I itch like everything! *(Jumps up and down and around the stage.)*

FARMER BARNWELL: I hear you were at the Spider Web Cafe.

Young artist with her decorated Frogette.

BULLY FROG: *(Stops jumping.)* Yes, I was, but never again! The racket of the singer named Flame hurt my ears, and the dancing for hours burned my webbed feet to a cinder. Worst of all, the most awful, terrible critter, named Crusher, the snapping turtle, tried to have my frog legs for dinner.

FARMER BARNWELL: Don't say I didn't warn you.

BULLY FROG: Next time I'll listen to your advice, Farmer Barnwell.

FARMER BARNWELL: Thank you, my young froggie friend. I'm glad to hear it. I'll be getting home for dinner now. *(Exits.)*

*(*LILY FROG *enters, dragging* MONSTER MOSQUITO *behind her.)*

BULLY FROG: Wow! A monster mosquito!

BOGGY WOG: Lily! Did you catch that monster mosquito all by yourself?

LILY FROG: I did.

BOGGY WOG: Where did you catch it?

LILY FROG: At the south end of the pond.

BULLY FROG: Gurrump! How about a date, Lily Frog? You can cook some mosquito meat for me.

Puppeteer with two Monster Mosquitoes.

LILY FROG: Go jump on your own lily pad and croak away, Bully Frog. No mosquito meat for you. I'm saving this for a rainy day. *(Exits, dragging the* MONSTER MOSQUITO *behind her.)*

BOGGY WOG: Gurrump! What a frog!

BULLY FROG: You said it.

Curtain.

Props: Music to play from backstage for Spider Web Cafe scene; lily pads (see instructions on pages 141–143).

See instructions for making frog and Monster Mosquito puppets on pages 125–141.

Production notes: You will need two Monster Mosquitoes: one on a wire to be "flown" around stage, and one on a string that can be attached to Lily Frog so she can drag it across the stage. You may wish to make the two mosquitoes with different color heads.

A nice touch for the Spider Web Cafe backdrop is a black spider web with a spider in it (see photo). Such webs are usually available at stores as Halloween party decorations.

How to Make Froggie Wog Stick Puppets

Photocopy or trace the patterns on the following pages. You have your choice of dressed or undressed versions, depending on how creative you feel. Decorate them with paints, crayons, sequins, glitter — have fun! Cut them out, lay them on sturdy cardboard, and trace their shapes onto the cardboard. Cut out the cardboard shapes and glue one end of a tongue depressor to each. Glue the decorated paper puppets onto the cardboard shapes with the tongue depressors sandwiched between.

Boggy Wog

Bully Frog

Mosquito-Bitten Bully Frog

Flame

Crusher

Zapper

Frogette

Lily Frog

Boggy Wog

Bully Frog

Flame

Zapper

Frogette

Lily Frog

How to Make a Monster Mosquito

1. Mark 2 big eyes on a large wooden bead. Color the rest of it black with a marker. This is your mosquito's head. Set aside.

2. Cut a clear plastic straw to 4". This will be your mosquito's body. If you don't have a clear straw, color straw to match mosquito's head.

3. Mark the straw with dots beginning ½" from the front end and then at ¼" spaces 4 more times. You will have 10 holes, five on each side of the straw. Put a hole in both sides of the straw with a push pin. You can do both sides at the same time, by squishing the straw.

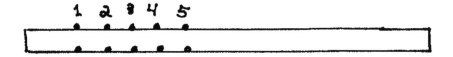

4. The second and third holes are for the wings. Take a 12" piece of 20-gauge wire and put it through both #2 holes, and push through so the straw is at the center of the wire. Take the right end of the wire and insert into the #3 hole on the right. Take the left end of the wire and insert into the #3 hole on the left.

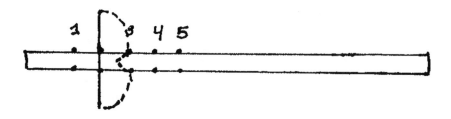

Place the wings flat on the table. Cover both wings with clear cellophane tape. Turn mosquito over and do the same on the other side. Trim tape edges.

5. Take another 12" piece of wire and put through both #1 holes, and push through so the straw is at the center of the wire. Do the same with more wire for #4 and #5 holes. These are the three pairs of legs.

To make sure legs stay in place, bend the right wires under the straw toward the left side and the left wires under the straw toward the right.

6. Put a 12" pipe cleaner through the straw. Put the head on the end of the pipe cleaner. Bend excess pipe cleaner down at the back of the mosquito. This will be the handle.

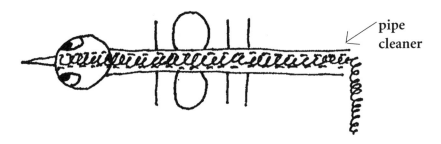

pipe cleaner

7. Put a toothpick into the front hole of the mosquito head. Leave about ¾" showing. Use a dab of glue to keep it in place, if needed.

8. Bend wings up a little, bend legs up a little, and then down and out.

How to Make Lily Pads

Photocopy or trace drawings of leaves and flowers on the following pages. The leaves are the flat, roughly heart-shaped part. Color these first in a light green, then streak on darker green. Color the flowers bright yellow. Cut out all pieces. Glue a strip of cardboard to each flower and glue the other end onto a leaf with the flower face down. Bend flower back and it will stand up on the leaf.

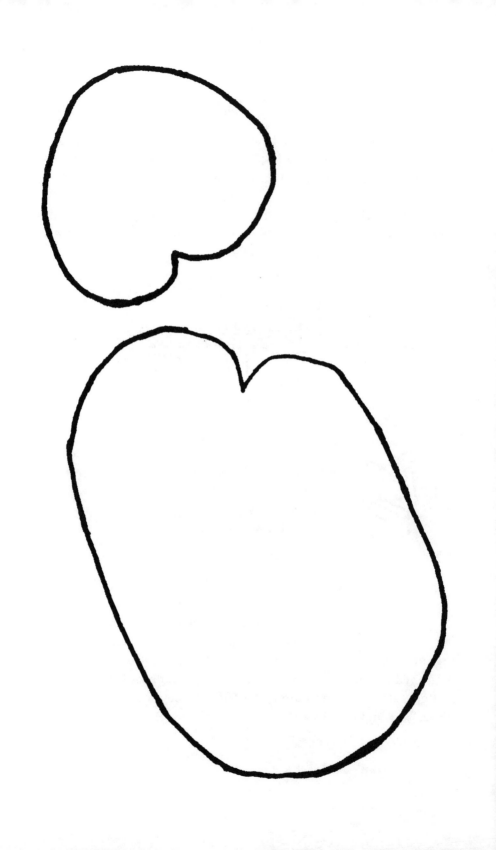

Talkabout

1. Why are most frogs green?
   (They blend into their surroundings.)
2. Why do frogs have long, sticky tongues?
   (To catch flying insects.)
3. Why do frogs want to catch insects?
   (Insects are their main food.)
4. What are tadpoles?
   (Baby frogs.)
5. Lots of people like to eat frog legs. They taste something like chicken. Have you ever eaten frog legs?
6. Have you seen or been in a frog jumping contest?
7. Have you ever played leap frog?
8. Why do they call the game leap frog?
   (Because one person leaps over another like a leaping frog.)
9. Frogs sing the loudest in the spring. Did you ever hear the frogs tuning up in a pond in the spring?
10. Who are the frogs' enemies?
    (Snakes, big birds, fishermen. Fishermen use frogs for bait and food.)
11. Why did Bully Frog want to leave home?
    (He thought Frog Pond was too dull, not exciting.)
12. Have you ever felt like leaving home?
13. Did Bully Frog find out home is best?
    (Yes.)
14. What happened to him?
    (He was bitten over and over by a monster mosquito.)
15. Who told Bully Frog not to go to the Spider Web Cafe?
    (Farmer Barnwell.)
16. Have you ever gone somewhere when you were told not to go?
17. Do you think it is a good idea to listen to older people? Why?
    (They have lived longer and been down the road before.)
18. What's a bullfrog?
    (The largest frog in the United States.)
19. Are you a Bully Frog or a Boggy Wog?
20. What's the difference in those two frog characters?

The Computer

WHERE: Farmer Barnwell's library. WHEN: Winter, one week after Christmas. PUPPETS: Seven. TIME: Approximately 10 minutes.

CHARACTERS

FARMER BARNWELL. . . Owns the Barnwell Farm
MARTHA BARNWELL . . His wife
ROSIE BARNWELL. . . . Farmer Barnwell's daughter
          (twin to Daisy)
DAISY BARNWELL. . . . Farmer Barnwell's daughter
          (twin to Rosie)
BUD BARNWELL . . . . The older Barnwell boy
BOBBY BARNWELL . . . The younger Barnwell boy
WATCHDOG . . . . . . Barnwells' dog

At Rise: FARMER BARNWELL is seated at his computer, which is placed to one side of the stage. The backdrop shows shelves of books with titles on them. Be sure a "Computer Book" is there. WATCHDOG is seated center stage.

———————————

FARMER BARNWELL: *(Jumps up and down and shouts.)* Hey! Hey! Hey! I'm Farmer Barnwell. Hot diggity dog, diggity dog, diggity dog, diggity dog. I'm a computer whiz!

WATCHDOG: *(Barks loudly.)* Arf! Arf!

MARTHA BARNWELL: *(Enters and goes to Farmer Barnwell.)* I'm glad you like the computer I gave you for Christmas, Harry, dear.

145

Watchdog, Farmer Barnwell and Martha shiver in their blankets in *The Computer.*

FARMER BARNWELL: Do I ever, Martha. The best present you ever gave me. I've got my program set up. You can give me a mouse for my birthday.

MARTHA BARNWELL: A mouse, Harry? I have enough mice scampering around the farm.

FARMER BARNWELL: *(Sighs.)* Computer talk is far too complicated for you to understand. I'm talking about a computer mouse. I can use it to change lines, move things around, and ever so many things.

MARTHA BARNWELL: The children know how to work a computer. Remember, you promised they could do their homework on your computer.

FARMER BARNWELL: Sure, I remember, but it's Christmas vacation and it's *my* Christmas present, so it's *my* computer time now.

WATCHDOG: Arf! Arf!

MARTHA BARNWELL: I'm glad you're happy. Have fun. *(Exits.)*

FARMER BARNWELL: I am having a ball. Hot diggity dog, diggity dog. Hey! Hey! *(Works at the computer.)*

WATCHDOG: Arf! Arf!

(ROSIE *and* DAISY *enter.*)

ROSIE: Dad, when are you going to let us use your computer?

FARMER BARNWELL: Later, Rosie. Later, Daisy.

DAISY: Always later. You promised to help us build a big snowman.

FARMER BARNWELL: Later, girls, later.

WATCHDOG: Arf! Arf!

ROSIE: Always later.

DAISY: You're no fun since you got your computer.

(ROSIE *and* DAISY *exit.*)

FARMER BARNWELL: (*Works at his computer, jumping up and down.*)
Hot diggity dog. I am a computer nut. Yes, I am. I'm a computer whiz.
Yes, I am.

WATCHDOG: Arf! Arf!

BUD: (*Enters.*) Dad, you're a computer nut.

FARMER BARNWELL: (*Doesn't answer. He sings.*) Hot diggity dog.
Hey! Hey!

BUD: (*Louder.*) Dad!

FARMER BARNWELL: (*Still doesn't answer. Keeps singing.*) Hot diggity dog!

BUD: (*Yells.*) Dad!

FARMER BARNWELL: (*Disgustedly.*) What do you want, Bud?

BUD: (*Talks fast.*) Miss Moo needs milking; the chickens are lay-
ing eggs all over the place, and we are out of wood for the fireplaces and
the wood stove; and —

FARMER BARNWELL: (*Sternly.*) You are a big boy, Bud. Go and take
care of it.

BUD: But, Dad!

FARMER BARNWELL: You heard me, Bud.

BUD: I can't do *everything* myself.

BOBBY: (*Enters very fast.*) Dad! Dad!

FARMER BARNWELL: (*Annoyed.*) What is it, Bobby? Can't you see I
am at the computer?

BOBBY: Dad, we've got to talk.

FARMER BARNWELL: I can't talk now, Bobby. Computer work, you
know. (*Jumps up and down.*) I'm working the keyboard of this computer like a master computer whiz.

BOBBY: But, Dad!

BUD: Dad, the roof is starting to leak. The animals are all upset and so is your family. We never see you any more since you got that computer. The driveway needs plowing. There's so much snow we can't get the truck out of the lower barn, so we can't go to the store for groceries. There's not much to eat in the house. We are freezing and starving.

BOBBY: That's what I was going to say.

FARMER BARNWELL: Go put on some sweaters and leave me be! *(Sings.)* Hot diggity dog, diggity dog. I've had a breakthrough!

BUD: I wish you had never seen a computer.

BOBBY: Me too.

(BUD and BOBBY exit.)

WATCHDOG: *(Goes to Farmer Barnwell.)* Arf! Arf! Hungry. Arf! Arf!

FARMER BARNWELL: Don't bother a computer whiz, Watchdog. Get lost.

WATCHDOG: *(Sadly walks to other side of stage. He looks back at Farmer Barnwell and barks.)* Arf! Arf! *(Exits.)*

(Curtain closes.)

SCENE 2

(Curtain opens. Same set as Scene 1 in the Barnwell's library. Farmer Barnwell has a blanket around his shoulders. Watchdog is center stage with a blanket around him. He sneezes.)

FARMER BARNWELL: I've been a month at the computer. I've got all my files in order. Hot diggity dog!

WATCHDOG: *(Sneezes.)* Arf! Arf!

FARMER BARNWELL: Watch my procedure, Watchdog. I'm great!

WATCHDOG: *(Sneezes.)* Arf! Arf!

MARTHA BARNWELL: *(Enters, wearing a blanket. She shivers.)* HAAAArrrry! Harry Barnwell, this computer business has gone too far. Your family and animals are cold and hungry. You have gone computer crazy. You hardly ever leave the computer. You fall asleep at that machine and never come to bed. You don't eat anything but a few crackers. You are losing weight. You are getting no exercise. Think of your health, Harry. Think of us, Harry. Your family needs you. Harry, I've had it! You've got to pull the plug on that contraption. It's got to go!

FARMER BARNWELL: I will, Martha, dear, as soon as I finish this program and store the information to save like I did before.

MARTHA BARNWELL: You'd better *save* this farm and family!

FARMER BARNWELL: Yes, Martha, dear.

WATCHDOG: *(Agrees.)* Arf! Arf!

*(*MARTHA BARNWELL *exits. Curtain closes.)*

SCENE 3

(Curtain opens. Same scene in library. Farmer Barnwell is still at his computer. Watchdog is still center stage. They have blankets around them. Farmer Barnwell moves and speaks slowly as he works at the keyboard.)

FARMER BARNWELL: H-o-t d-i-g-g-i-t-y d-d-dog. Diggity doooog. I'm working soooo slowly. The computer knows more than I know, but I am the one who puts the info into it. I am a commm-puter whizzzz!

WATCHDOG: *(Barks slowly.)* A-A-A-Arf!

FARMER BARNWELL: *(Talks slowly.)* Let me see. I'm not seeing the computer very clearly. I must have the stare glare. My back is killing me. Now, where was I? Oh, yes. Man, I have a doozy of a headache—a computer headache, and I have a cold. *(Sniffs.)* Maybe the flu. My fingers are cramped, but I must keep pushing the keys.

WATCHDOG: *(Slowly.)* Arf! Arf!

FARMER BARNWELL: *(Starts talking slowly, then picks up speed.)* Farmer Barnwell's Farm Program. I have six chickens. My six hens lay three eggs a day. Eggs cost four dollars a dozen. I'd make six dollars a day. Cost of feed is sixty cents a day. If I buy six more hens, I'd make—

MARTHA BARNWELL: *(Enters with a blanket around her and her hat on her head.)* Harry Barnwell, you have been too long at that computer. I can't take another day of it. You're like a computer zombie. It's time to get the farm ready for spring.

FARMER BARNWELL: But I am a computer whiz.

MARTHA BARNWELL: You'd better whiz yourself away from that machine, or I'm leaving!

FARMER BARNWELL: Where are you going?

MARTHA BARNWELL: I'm taking the children and we are going to live at Catnip Lodge.

FARMER BARNWELL: *(Not looking up.)* That will be nice, dear. Have a good time.

MARTHA BARNWELL: *(Sadly.)* Oh, Harry! *(Exits.)*

FARMER BARNWELL: Oh, you beautiful keyboard. Boot it up. There's my menu. Hot diggity dog, diggity dog. Hey! Hey! I've gotten my second wind.

WATCHDOG: Arf! Arf!

FARMER BARNWELL: Where's that cursor? Hey! Hey! Put it on the hard drive. I love my work station. Man, do I have the computer jive. Hi-ho the dairy-o ... How many cows do I have? *(Calculates on computer.)* One. That's our Miss Moo.

(A sad mooing is heard offstage.)

WATCHDOG: *(Walks sadly off.)* Arf! Arf! Arf!

FARMER BARNWELL: How do you expect me to make good decisions on my computer with all this racket? I am all set to store my best work on the computer. I'll push the "save" button. *(He cries out loudly.)* Oh! No! Oh, no! No! No! No! My computer has had a blowout! The electricity must be off. I have lost my best programs. I'll have to start all over again. It's down the tubes. Oh, woe is me! *(He cries loudly. He stops crying and looks around.)* Where is everybody? Where is Martha? Where are the children? Where is Watchdog? Everybody is gone. *(Sadly.)* I am alone with my computer. A computer is great, but a computer is only a machine. Brrrrr. It's cold in here. I'm tired and hungry. Wonder how long I've been in a computer daze? I miss my family. If I get the farm running right again, maybe they will come home. Martha did say something about going to Catnip Lodge.

(MARTHA BARNWELL enters.)

FARMER BARNWELL: Martha! *(Runs painfully to her.)* Oh, my aching back! My aching head! My aching eyes!

MARTHA BARNWELL: Poor Harry! We couldn't stay away any longer. We love you, Harry. I wish I'd never given you that computer. How come you are not at the keyboard?

FARMER BARNWELL: The electricity was turned off. I blew my best programs.

MARTHA BARNWELL: That's because we couldn't pay the bill.

FARMER BARNWELL: I'll fix up the farm and take care of the animals, and the children will have turns at the computer.

Farmer Barnwell and friend at the computer.

MARTHA BARNWELL: That's the way to talk, Harry. Now you're my old Harry again.

FARMER BARNWELL: There's plenty of time for computer work after I get my chores done. Besides, once this farm gets moving again, I can save up enough money to buy a mouse, more disks and new programs. Then I can redo the program I lost!

MARTHA BARNWELL: *(Sitting down at computer.)* Maybe when I'm finished, Harry. Hot diggity dog, diggity dog! I'm going on the Internet! *(She types away as the curtain closes.)*
Curtain.

Props: Blankets for Farmer Barnwell, Martha and Watchdog; hat for Martha; computer.

See instructions for making Watchdog on pages 108–110. See instructions for making computer on pages 152–153.

Production notes: Burlap makes a good backdrop. Glue or sew on long strips of felt crossways for shelves. Use shorter strips to make books "standing" on shelves with spines showing. You can use markers or stick-on letters to put titles on the spines. (One should say "Computer Book.")

How to Make a Computer

Computer monitor: Using cardboard or posterboard, cut two pieces 3½" × 2¾" (front and back); two pieces 2¾" × 1½" (sides); and two pieces 3½" × 1½" (top and bottom). Tape into a box shape. Cut a 2" × 1¾" hole in front and glue or tape paper on inside for the screen.

Hard drive: Cut two pieces 2¼" × 4" (top and bottom); two pieces 4" × ¾" (front and back); and two pieces 2¼" × 2¼" (sides). Tape into a box shape and place under monitor. Draw slot for imaginary disk.

Keyboard: Cut two pieces ¾" × 4½" (back and top). On one of these pieces, draw a typewriter keyboard. Cut two squares of cardboard or posterboard, ¾" × ¾"; cut across top of each at an angle to make slanted sides for keyboard. Tape back, top, and sides together. Add a strip measuring ¼" by 4½" to front.

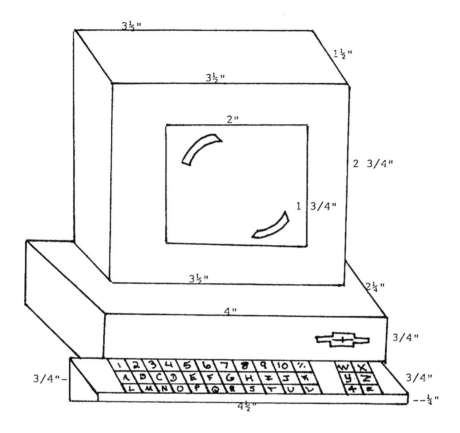

Talkabout

1. Did Farmer Barnwell like his computer?
   (Yes.)
2. Did he like his computer too much?
   (Yes.)
3. How do you know?
   (He let his farm go to pieces and never had time for his family.)
4. Did the Barnwell children know how to use the computer?
   (Yes. They asked to use the computer to do their homework.)
5. Do you know how to use a computer? Do you like using a computer?
6. Can you do something so much that you end up in trouble?
   (Yes.)

7. What trouble did Farmer Barnwell get himself into by using the computer all the time?

> (He made himself sick with backaches, headaches, eyeaches. He didn't feed the animals or take care of his family.)

8. Are computers good?

> (Emphasize that computers are useful when used properly.)

9. What are some of the things you can do on a computer?

> (Make music, make movies, make drawings, do book reports, find information, make friends…)

10. Do you help your Mom and Dad to learn how to use a computer?

Writing Your Own
Old Barn Puppet Play

Now that you are a puppeteer, how about trying your hand in writing a puppet play? I bet you can come up with a good play. Here is how to get started:

Think up which puppet in the book you would like for your main character, or make up your own character. Give the puppet a name. Think about your character puppet. Is he or she old or young? How does he or she talk, walk, think, act? Give your puppet something that stands out; for example, maybe he sneezes all the time (hay fever!). Decide where the play will take place. Where does your puppet live? Who is in his family?

Now choose another puppet who makes trouble for your main character. The play can be funny or serious, but either way, give it lots of action. Plan everything out first. Write it down or at least know the ideas you want to put across in your play.

Don't use too many puppets. Get your audience's attention right away. Work your ideas along, and tie up the action with a good ending. Did your puppet character change in any way by the time the play ended?

You can work alone or with a partner, both in writing the play and presenting the play. Practice your play so you know what you are doing. If you have the ideas, you can make up the words as you go, but writing the words down is safer. Either way, you'll become a real playwright.

Some people are better at making puppets, some are better at working the puppets, and some are better at writing puppet plays. Try it all. The world of puppetry is a wonderful world.